Bloom's

GUIDES

Stephen Crane's
Maggie: A Girl of the Streets

1984
The Adventures of Huckleberry Finn
All the Pretty Horses
Beloved
Brave New World
The Chosen
The Crucible
Cry, the Beloved Country
Death of a Salesman
The Grapes of Wrath
Great Expectations
Hamlet
The Handmaid's Tale
The House on Mango Street
I Know Why the Caged Bird Sings
The Iliad
Lord of the Flies
Macbeth
Maggie: A Girl of the Streets
The Member of the Wedding
Pride and Prejudice
Ragtime
Romeo and Juliet
The Scarlet Letter
Snow Falling on Cedars
A Streetcar Named Desire
The Things They Carried
To Kill a Mockingbird

Bloom's
GUIDES

Stephen Crane's
Maggie: A Girl of the Streets

Edited & with an Introduction
by Harold Bloom

CHELSEA HOUSE
P U B L I S H E R S
A Haights Cross Communications ◀ Company
Philadelphia

First Printing
1 3 5 7 9 8 6 4 2

Library of Congress Cataloging-in-Publication Data
Bloom, Harold.
    Maggie : a girl of the streets / edited & with an introduction by
Harold Bloom.
            p. cm. -- (Bloom's guides)
    Includes bibliographical references and index.
    ISBN 0-7910-7879-5 (alk. paper)
1. Crane, Stephen, 1871-1900. Maggie, a girl of the streets. 2.
Prostitutes in literature. I. Title. II. Series.
    PS1449.C85M333 2004
813'.4--dc22
                                    2004015597

Contributing editor: Janyce Marson
Cover design by Takeshi Takahashi
Layout by EJB Publishing Services

Contents

 Introduction

As in his masterpiece, *The Red Badge of Courage* (1895), Stephen Crane relies upon pure imagination in composing his first narrative fiction, *Maggie: A Girl of the Streets* (1893). Crane had never seen a battle when he wrote *The Red Badge of Courage*, and he scarcely had encountered the low life of the Bowery before he produced *Maggie*. Ironically, he was to have all too much of slum life after *Maggie* was printed, and to see more than enough bloodshed as a war correspondent, after *The Red Badge of Courage* had made him famous.

Maggie is a curious book to reread, partly because of its corrosive irony, but also it hurts to encounter again the over-determined ruin of poor Maggie. Her ghastly family, dreadful lover, and incessant poverty all drive her into prostitution and the ambiguous death by drowning, which may be suicide or victimage by murder.

The minimal but authentic aesthetic dignity of *Maggie* results from the strangeness so frequently characteristic of Nineteenth-century realism and naturalism. Zola, whose influence seems strong in *Maggie*, actually created a visionary naturalism, more phantasmagoric than realistic. Crane, impressionist and ironist, goes even further in *Maggie*, a laconic experiment in word-painting. Crane's imagery is Hogarthian yet modified by an original perspectivism, irrealistic and verging upon surrealism. Maggie herself is an uncanny prophecy of what was to be the central relationship of Crane's brief life, his affair with Cora Taylor, who ran a bordello in Jacksonville, Florida. She accompanied him to England, where their friends included Joseph Conrad and Henry James, and she sustained him through the agony of his early death.

7

Biographical Sketch

At two o'clock in the morning on September 16, 1896, while walking along Sixth Avenue in New York with two chorus girls, Stephen Crane witnessed a policeman arresting these two young women on the fabricated charge that they were attempting to solicit two men. One of these women, Dora Clark, was imprisoned that same night—calling out to Crane that she wanted to appear before the magistrate. While she may not have been soliciting at the time of her arrest, the sergeant was willing to charge her because he knew her to be a common prostitute. Crane decided to become her advocate and challenge the New York City Police Department. The following morning, Crane waited inside the Jefferson Market Courthouse until he could address the judge and proclaim Dora's innocence. A reporter from the *New York Journal* observed what transpired, not realizing that Crane was a well-known writer. He documented his observations and, on September 17, the Stephen Crane story had made headlines all over New York—the *New York Journal* proclaimed, "He Wore No Red Badge of Courage, But Pluckily Saved a Girl from the Law." By the next day, September 18, the favorable publicity bestowed on Crane took on a decidedly negative tone with such newspapers as the *Chicago Dispatch* stating that his "association with women in scarlet is not necessarily a 'Red Badge of Courage.'"

Coincidentally, it was also at this time that Crane's publisher, S.S. McClure, introduced him to the New York City Police Commissioner, Theodore Roosevelt (who would later become President of the United States only a few years after Crane's death). McClure was considering having Crane write a story about the New York police. Roosevelt, a strong advocate of police reform ever since his campaign in 1895, had felt "demoralized by the ... venality and blackmail" within the department. When Roosevelt first made Crane's acquaintance, he was a great admirer of his work, especially *The Red Badge of Courage*, and owned all of Crane's books. Both he and Crane shared a love of books, especially of Tolstoy and stories of the West and the hard-riding cowboys. In August of that year, Crane sent Roosevelt an autographed copy of *George's Mother*. Nevertheless, whatever positive feelings Roosevelt may have had for Crane and his work soon changed following Crane's impolitic response to an unfortunate public event.

During that same August, William Jennings Bryan was in the midst of campaigning as the Democratic candidate for the presidency at Madison Square Garden when a security fiasco took place. Gatecrashers arrived in force leaving legitimate ticket holders unable to attend the event. The affair received much bad publicity from the press. Although Roosevelt wrote to Crane in an attempt to excuse the police on grounds of inexperience with this type of mob, it is unclear whether Crane ever received his letter. Crane wrote a scathing article in the August 20 edition of the *Gazette*, referring to the police department's mismanagement as a "shameful performance" while lauding the former and very corrupt police chief, Thomas F. Byrnes. Crane's criticism did not end there. In his August 27 column, Crane again attacked Roosevelt—this time for his rigid enforcement of the blue laws which he believed led to the police department's persecution of the city's harmless traders. In response to his vitriol, the New York City police set to work trying to gather as much incriminating evidence about Crane's character. Their efforts included a raid on his apartment as well as attempts at proving his consorting with chorus girls and prostitutes. Roosevelt, a man of impossibly high moral standards, would come to view Stephen Crane as objectionable for displaying a distressing lack of propriety.

It was also during the summer of 1896 that Crane lived with Amy Leslie, the well-known drama critic of the *Chicago Daily News*, at 121 West 27th Street. Though she was Crane's senior by 16 years, she was considered to be a very beautiful woman. Her photographs always depicted her as being elaborately dressed with a beautiful smile. Leslie led a glamorous life attending theater openings and parties, and she was considered to be brilliant and witty, at times demonstrating a very sharp tongue. Having started out as an actress and singer herself,

9

Leslie was known to be nurturing towards actors and generous in her reviews. At the time she met Crane, she may still have been married to the comedian Harry Brown. After their summer together Leslie returned to her apartment in Chicago—the couple continued to see each other when they could. Only Crane's side of the correspondence between the two lovers still exists and, from those letters, it is apparent that Leslie was in some kind of trouble. Believing that she would return to New York to live with Crane after his return from Cuba, she entrusted him with eight hundred dollars, which he was to deposit in a bank in New York. Crane, taking the easier course, apparently put her money in his own account. Leslie was enraged at his casual handling of her money. Leslie's letters soon indicated that she knew Crane had taken with a new lover—accusations Crane would flatly deny though he knew their romance was over.

Later in that year, while on his way to cover the insurrection against Spanish rule in Cuba, Crane stopped in Jacksonville, Florida, which at that time had become the country's major filibustering port. American sympathies towards the Cuban insurgents were high, having been inflamed by the yellow journalism of Hearst's *New York Journal* and Joseph Pulitzer's *New York World*. Along with the strong sympathy, there was also the potential to make money by smuggling arms to the insurgents. Stephen Crane was of the belief that the idea of smuggling arms was romantically appealing for clandestine activities, referring to it as a "delicious bit of outlawry in the evening of the nineteenth century." Upon his arrival in Jacksonville, Crane registered at the best hotel under the alias Samuel Carleton. While visiting the smoky back rooms of seedy waterfront saloons and local brothels he met Cora Taylor, six years his senior, and the proprietress of her aptly named Hotel de Dream. At 31, Taylor prided herself on looking young. Like his former sweetheart, Amy Leslie, Cora was short, blond, and attractive and her manner of dressing suggested an affluent way of life. Interestingly, Taylor came from a fine and very literate family in Boston. Her paternal great grandfather had been a prominent Boston art dealer, her father was a painter and, thus, she had been raised in an atmosphere of artistic appreciation. Following her parents' death, which left her a wealthy young woman, Cora soon departed from the mores of her social background. At not yet twenty years of age, Cora lived out of wedlock with a man while working as a hostess at a gambling house, the London Club, followed by two brief and unsuccessful marriages. A well-known personality in Jacksonville, and an intriguing woman who had a mixture of scandal and propriety about her, Cora ran her "sporting house" as an elegant establishment. She even had a man called Professor to play the piano for her "guests." Stephen Crane would meet her at a dinner party shortly after his arrival in Jacksonville, and it was at this time he revealed Samuel Carleton's true identity. Cora was delighted to make Crane's acquaintance as she had been reading one of his books, which were very much in vogue at that time. He would live with Cora for the last three years of his life. Crane's preference for a woman like Cora, is characteristic of his own rebellious personality and, further, of the lives of the socially-marginalized urban poor whom he observed and subsequently wrote about.

Indeed, Stephen Crane was forever resistant to his parents' strict religious beliefs and traditional notions of social propriety. Born on November 1, 1871 in Newark, New Jersey, Stephen was the son of a Methodist preacher, the Reverend Johnathan Townley Crane, who had once described mankind's condition as "one of inexpressible evil," destined to a hell of "eternal darkness and despair." Awarded a doctorate of divinity from Dickinson College in 1856, Reverend Crane wrote numerous articles and books declaiming the evils of dancing, novel reading, and intoxication. Though he was against slavery, he wanted to avoid a civil war and, thus, proposed a system of serfdom, similar to that of Russia. Stephen, on the other hand, though of a gentle temperament, would later become obsessed by war and violence culminating in the writing of his greatest novel, *The Red Badge of Courage*. His mother, Mary Helen Peck Crane was a kindly and devout woman who, although reconciled to the life of a minister's wife, including a series of frequent moves, nevertheless loved to paint and believed that she should be doing a lot more than household chores. As the mother of fourteen children, Stephen being the last, her responsibilities were endless.

Because his health was fragile as a child, there is a discrepancy among biographers as to when he started school. The authors of *The Crane Log* maintain that he began school in January, 1880 at the Mountain House School in Port Jervis, New York after an abbreviated start at the Main Street School. When his father died in February, 1880, Mrs. Crane and her younger children were required to leave the parsonage and eventually took up residence in Asbury Park, New Jersey some three years later. Asbury Park, a proud prohibition town, proved to be a haven for American Methodists in that it provided a safe refuge from life's temptations. It is here, in 1883, that Stephen enrolled in the sixth grade at the Asbury Park School, and where he writes his first known story, "Uncle Jake and the Bell Handle," a tale of two country bumpkins on a day's outing in the big city. On September 14, 1885, Stephen enrolls at his father's old school, Pennington Seminary, a rigid, coeducational boarding school just north of Trenton, an institution primarily intended to prepare young men for the seminary.

By the time Crane enrolled at Syracuse University in January 1891, he had already decided on a literary career. After moving into a spacious second-floor apartment with his roommate, Clarence N. Goodwin, Crane joined several clubs, among them the Nut-Brown Maiden, a coasting club; an eating group called the Tooth Pick Club, and Delta Upsilon's cricket club where he served as captain. Though he was of slight build, he immediately tried out for the baseball team, a game which he enjoyed playing since childhood, and for which he was already a legendary catcher. The Syracuse team was considered middling, but Crane was considered the best player of nine and one of the best catchers in Syracuse's history. Crane's scholastic achievements, however, were far from remarkable. He was a student of his own invention, registering for only one course, English literature, in the College of Liberal Arts. He preferred to relax in his room, reading newspapers, history books and literary masterpieces, among them *Faust, Anna Karenina*, and *War and Peace*. On June 12, 1891, Crane left Syracuse, declaring college to be "a waste of time." It was around this time that he began his career in journalism and immersed himself in the kind of lifestyle of which he was asked to write.

On the morning of August 17, 1892, Crane attended a lecture on the novelist William Dean Howells, delivered by Hamlin Garland, a young teacher from Boston and rising literary star. Crane listened with rapt attention to Garland's theory of realism in art and literature, which essentially held the view that true art must reflect contemporary American life in all its variety. In the following years, a great friendship evolved, with Garland and Crane discussing their two great passions—literature and baseball. In October of that year, Crane began making frequent trips to New York City, exploring the tenements, the Bowery, the saloons and dance halls, the brothels and flophouses. It was the world of the marginalized and dispossessed. It was also during this time that his mother died at the age of sixty-four. Crane had just turned twenty and, in the months following his mother's death, he wrote his *Sullivan County Tales* about four hapless men, innocents and social misfits, who wander through a mountainous forest, disconnected from the outside world. It is in these sketches that Crane makes full use of color as metaphor and dream imagery to express the unconscious mind. However, after a few jobs with New York newspapers, Crane lived a life of privation, moving into various seedy apartments with his artist friends. As a result of his own experience with poverty, and having received an assignment from the newly-formed Bacheller-Johnson Newspaper Syndicate to write about the Bowery, in 1893 Crane was asked to live amongst and write "An Experiment in Misery," a story about the sordid life of a flophouse, replete with "strange and unspeakable odors." It was an assignment which Crane relished and was an experiment in living which he had no trouble adapting to. Shortly thereafter, Crane wrote, and published at his own expense, *Maggie: A Girl of the Streets*.

However, although both Hamlin Garland and W.D. Howells admired the novel, it did not sell, and it is generally agreed among critics that the audience of the 1890's was looking for escapist fiction which would provide a distraction from the social and moral issues of the day. Crane's next literary endeavor would be his masterpiece, *The Red Badge of Courage*, where he would use the Civil War as his subject. As a story about the education and growth into manhood of the young Henry Fleming, it is a narrative which builds on several major literary traditions ranging from Homer to Shakespeare, and Herman Melville among others. It is a story in which personal identity is complex and ambiguous and, in this capacity, it is very modern. Crane's fortunes began to improve immediately when "Red Badge" was first published as a syndicated newspaper story in December, 1894. That same newspaper hired Crane in 1895 to be a reporter in the American West and Mexico, an experience which lead to his writing "The Bridge Comes to Yellow Sky" and "The Blue Hotel." When *The Red Badge* appeared in book form in the fall of 1895, Crane received international acclaim at the age of 24.

On December 29, 1899, following a ball at which such literary greats as Henry James, H.G. Wells, George Gissing, and Joseph Conrad were guests, Stephen Crane suffered a lung hemorrhage which he tried to conceal from Cora. Crane continued to work from bed and in early February, 1900, he was busy writing chapter after chapter of a new swashbuckling novel about an Irish blade named the O'Ruddy. Stephen Crane died on June 5, 1900. That same day, he had dictated more of his romance, now entitled *The O'Ruddy*, a narrative filled with the action of men galloping on horses through a Sussex rain. As Cora wrote in her notebook, Stephen was glad that she had cut his hair "during illness so that he would not be a bald old man."

The Story Behind The Story

The story behind the origins of Stephen Crane's *Maggie: A Girl of the Streets* is as turbulent and precarious as its portrayal of the destructive nature of urban life in the 1890s Bowery. While working as a reporter during the summer of 1892 on the Asbury Park beat, Stephen Crane met a young and beautiful married woman, a few years older than he, named Lily Brandon Monroe. Her husband, Hersey Munroe, was a successful and prosperous geologist. At the time she met Stephen Crane, Lily was staying at the Lake Avenue Hotel while her husband was away on a Geological Survey trip. Though the frail, melancholic and oddly prudish Crane would appear to be an unlikely suitor, Lily loved him for his brilliance and idealism. For his part, Crane was enchanted with Lily and relished the gossiping old ladies at the hotel who were shocked at the scandalous nature of their relationship. When Crane tried to impress Lily's father by speaking in French, Mr. Munroe quickly put a stop to the affectation, stating that his daughter did not speak French. Crane went so far as to propose marriage, but she ultimately declined. He had also given Lily a manuscript of his street-girl novel and when Lily's husband found out about the affair, he destroyed the manuscript.

In the fall of 1892, without any job prospects, Stephen Crane moved into a cheap apartment in New York City with a group of medical students. Located at 1064 Avenue A, between the Bowery and the East River, it was the world of the marginalized and dispossessed. And its forms of entertainment and distraction were equally as tawdry, consisting of saloons, dance halls, brothels and flophouses. However, his roommates were young and optimistic, and romanticized their surroundings by referring to the apartment as the Pendennis Club (in all probability a reference to Thackeray's novel of a spoiled young snob who wrote novels). It was here that Crane continued to work on *Maggie*, a story of the seduction and abandonment of an impoverished Irish girl, set in the fictional world of Rum Alley. Anxious to see *Maggie* in print, Crane was advised that the profanity and vulgarity of speech in his novel would make it difficult for him to find a publisher.

During this time, Crane was also forced to contend with the very real hardships of his own impoverished life. "While *Maggie's* fate lay undecided, winter arrived with a vengeance. One night Crane and Phil May, a British artist and illustrator, borrowed a tiger skin belonging to illustrator William Francis 'Frank' Ver Beck. A policeman found them under the skin, walking up and down Broadway at 3:30 a.m., and brought them into the Tenderloin station. He released the young men but kept the skin." (Davis, 56–57) By January 1893, Crane had still not found a publisher, although the rejections were accompanied by praise for his work. Accordingly, upon the advice of Willis Fletcher Johnson, Crane resolved to publish *Maggie* anonymously, under the pseudonym Johnston Smith, at his own expense. Crane then sent copies to social reformers and editors, and Hamlin Garland, a writer and literary scholar, as well as a personal friend of his. Crane's friends also devised their own schemes for getting his name into the public domain. His "friends tried to help sales by conspicuously reading copies in the elevated train 'so that passengers would think the metropolis was Maggie-mad.'..." (Davis, 59) In fact, in their enthusiasm to help the young novelist, his roommates threw a party designed to promote his book. "On the night of the party, in late February or early March, *Maggies* lined the wall, held up the wassail punch bowl, filled in the empty spaces where furniture should have been." (Davis, 59) The party eventually became rowdy, causing the landlady to complain. But, despite all the fanfare and his friends' best efforts, Crane was left discouraged about the lack of interest in his book.

By the time Stephen Crane arrived in New York City, the Bowery had become a notorious hangout for New York's gangsters in the 1890s, often referred to as a den of vice and dissipation. In his description of the cheap flop houses which proliferated in the seventies and eighties, Harlow states that the newly-arrived and unsuspecting boarders, along with the downtrodden regulars, were easy prey for the Bowery crooks. "Here the crook or the fence, looking for allies, found them more readily than did the missionary, and the lodging houses became nurseries of crime. It was calculated in 1890 that nine thousand homeless young men lodged nightly along Park Row and the Bowery...." (Harlow, 407) In its more prosperous days, the Bowery had been one of New York's most elegant streets at the end of the 18th century. After a fire in 1835 destroyed most of the old Dutch townhouses, the Bowery lost much of its elegant charm. By the Civil War, beer gardens and the like had replaced the mansions and shops in the neighborhood. At the middle of the century, after the Astor Place Riot of 1849, many of the more exclusive enterprises moved uptown, leaving the Bowery to become known for cheap trade and entertainment.

The Entertainments of "Rum Alley"

For their first date, Pete takes Maggie to a beer-garden, "a great green-hued hall," where the clientele is comprised of factory workers and manual laborers, "people who showed that all day they strove with their hands." In his edition of *Maggie*, Thomas Gullason suggests that the specific locale is the most famous beer hall in New York, the Atlantic Garden, located at 50–54, the Bowery. Occupied on the site of an old factory and coal yard, the Atlantic Garden, established in 1858, was owned by the sons of William Kramer. It was a respectable establishment, bedecked with plants and flowers, and served up to four thousand customers an evening. Brooks McNamara describes the Atlantic Garden as a venue dedicated to family entertainment and allowing for no improprieties. As a testament to its propriety, the entertainment was likewise unobjectionable, and the women singers were well-trained and suitably dressed. "As a matter of fact, the Atlantic Garden seems to have specialized in rigidly proper female entertainers." (McNamara, 102) Citing James D. McCabe, Jr.'s *Lights and Shadows of New York Life, or, Sights and Sensations of the Great City*, McNamara includes the following description of the Atlantic Garden. "On an instant the orchestra breaks forth in some wonderful German melody, or some deep voiced, strong lunged singer sends his notes rolling through the hall. The auditors have suddenly lost their merriment, and are now listening pensively to the music, which is good." (McNamara, 102) The various forms of entertainment offered by the German beer garden also included dancing, comedy, opera singers as well as popular singers and mechanical music. As a social phenomenon, the patrons of the 1890's beer halls reflected the ever-changing immigrant population. In the 1890s, German immigrants were the predominant group, with a population of 370,000 in New York City by 1880, and would remain so until 1900. The Bowery and the Lower East Side were referred to as "Kleindeutschland," where the rents were low and where there already existed a group of German-speaking inhabitants. Crane is careful to include this demographic detail in his description of the beer hall that Maggie and Pete attend. "Quiet Germans, with maybe their wives and two or three children, sat listening to the music, with the expressions of happy cows.... [while only] an occasional party of sailors from a war-ship, their faces pictures of sturdy health, spent the earlier hours of the evening at the small round tables." Nevertheless, the concert saloons that Pete takes Maggie to are devoid of the aforementioned respectability.

The other entertainments described in *Maggie* are likewise steeped in baseness and corruption. Crane makes numerous references to the many grotesque aspects of life in the Bowery, and the distractions offered to its unfortunate inhabitants consistently and emphatically underscore the inhumanity of the urban slum.

Although Crane does not specifically name them, between 1880 and 1900 dime museums were a flourishing business in the Bowery. The typical late nineteenth century New York City dime museum, with its ten cent admission fee, catered to a working-class and lower-middle-class clientele. Recalling the "cabinets of curiosities" that had been popular among the wealthy and learned elite in Europe during the Renaissance, dime museums capitalized on human and animal anomalies, the freak shows whose antecedents in America were the circus and P.T. Barnum's American Museum (1851), which, under the guise of entertainment and education, became the foremost venues of spectacle and popular culture. Dime museums also displayed everything from historical relics and wax figures to clever automatons. One feature that separated the dime museum from such genuine institutions as the Metropolitan Museum of Art was the dime museum's emphasis on live performance. The various freaks and working acts of the dime museum were guaranteed fifteen to twenty hours of work a week, and were often able to live a comfortable life in retirement. While their frequent exploitation cannot be overlooked, many freaks used personal exhibition as a means to financial security, education and meaningful self-expression. Far more than just a "freakery" or a circus, the dime museum of the late nineteenth century was an assortment of artifacts and curiosities from travel to exotic lands, dioramas, panoramas, stuffed animals and mechanical contraptions, a combination of popular entertainments and quasi-educational exhibits, all with a fair share of hoaxes as well. Worth and Huber's Palace Museum claimed to offer wholesome entertainment suitable for children and ladies with such bizarre attractions such "Jo-Jo, the Dog-Faced Boy," "Baby Bunting, the Smallest Living Horse," and Ajeeb, a mechanical chess player. (Dennett, 58) Though they would eventually vanish from the urban landscape, the exhibits and performances which took place at American dime museums continued to influence stage entertainment and traveling shows for years.

Typically housed in a two or three story structure, customers would buy a ticket and proceed to the top floor to view the permanent collection of artifacts. From there they would proceed to the second floor curio hall where freaks and circus acts were performed and, finally, to the ground floor which contained a theater offering a variety show. Other attractions were also available. "In many of the so-called medicine or anatomical museums on the Bowery, gullible patrons were lured into the office of the 'doctor' or 'professor' for blood pressure or lung tests, a phrenological examination, or a palm reading." (Dennet, 61) The agenda was to frighten the patron into requesting a cure, for which the patient would have to pay a considerable sum. To add to the scam, this hidden fee was never mentioned until the patron was already into the procedure he so desperately believed he now needed. A number of these "professors" were often disbarred physicians or untrained confidence men. (Dennet, 63) Dime museums were a class of cheap entertainment establishments against which 1890's tourists were warned categorically by the guide books. Indeed, Crane's disparaging comparison of Jimmie as a "glib showman at a museum" is a clear reference to the unsavory characters who owned or supervised these establishments. Devoid of human compassion, these entrepreneurs capitalized on other people's misfortune.

Essentially bars that presented low-cost shows to attract customers, concert saloons are another important cultural phenomenon of late 19th Century Bowery life and are important venues throughout *Maggie*. Chapters 10 and 14 present particularly frightening glimpses of the inherent danger and degradation of the Bowery concert saloon, evoking images of corruption and ultimate despair as they beckon seductively to passersby. A common feature of many of these establishments was the female waitress, mostly a part-time prostitute, who served drinks to male customers. Concert saloons featured variant forms of variety theatre, including an early form of burlesque, and performers from other types of establishments such as the dime museums, minstrel shows and circuses, became part of the saloon circuit. "Entertainers sang, danced, and played musical instruments, and often presented non-musical material—usually simply rhymes or couplets—as part of their acts." (McNamara, 51) In addition to these acts, a number of entertainers from the minstrel theatres introduced blackface songs and sketches, performing on banjos, bones, guitars and violin cellos. Although illegal, gymnastic acts also began to appear, as well as exhibition boxing matches. As the demographics of the Lower East Side changed during the last two decades of the nineteenth century, a new focus emerged regarding the objects of satire—specifically the Irish and Germans—the new immigrants of New York City. Nevertheless, while the variety of live performances increased with the passage of time, the proprietors of these establishments were primarily interested in turning a profit rather than becoming a platform for creativity in the theatrical arts.

Added to this lack of interest in artistic performance, concert saloons were notoriously involved in illegal activities. Accordingly, the physical structures which housed the concert saloon were generally shabby, with the owners and managers preferring cheap and unobtrusive quarters that kept their establishment in the shadows. "In the final analysis, the spaces in many concert saloons were probably fairly crude and badly adapted to performance—they were often an afterthought designed to turn an ordinary saloon into a theatre of a sort. But drinking remained the chief business of the concert saloon. Shows—like waiter girls—were a novelty designed to bring in customers." (McNamara, 76)

When Maggie and Pete are together on weekday evenings, they attend the conventional melodramatic plays so popular in the 1890's Bowery. Stephen Crane had a low opinion of these melodramas with their elaborate crises and overblown emotional displays in which a "brain-clutching heroine [is] rescued from the palatial home of her guardian." Maggie, on the other hand, is completely given over to sympathy for these exaggerated characters and plots. Tragically, she is laboring under the blind-sighted belief that she will be able to escape her poverty. "She rejoiced at the way in which the poor and virtuous eventually surmounted the wealthy and wicked."

The defining elements of melodrama, a genre that arose in the late 18th century, are an elaborate plot with many twists and turns selected for maximum stage spectacle, a clearly defined hero, and villainous characters. Melodramas packed theatres throughout the nineteenth century during a time when cities were growing rapidly and theatres were the most popular entertainment for the growing middle and working classes. The melodramas of the 19th Century mark the peak of popularity of live theatre, with more people attending the theatre than at any other time in western history. One of the largest theatres in New York, The Bowery, became known as "The Slaughterhouse" because of the gory spectacle that it frequently produced. Other enormously popular topics of melodrama were frontier stories, rags to riches stories, and stories about race relations.

Central Park

The Central Park Menagerie, which Pete and Maggie visit one Sunday, had an interesting history by the time Crane wrote *Maggie*. When the Park began to receive animals as gifts in the 1860s, some of the animals were tethered to poles outside the Arsenal. For a brief period, live animals were even kept in the basement. During this time, the British sculptor and educator, Benjamin Waterhouse Hawkins, had planned to construct a Paleozoic Museum featuring sculptured dinosaurs as a distinct institution within Central Park. After 1827, Hawkins devoted himself to the study of natural history, and in 1852 included the subject of geology. Mr. Hawkins was assistant superintendent of the World's fair in London in 1851 and, in 1852, was appointed by the Crystal Palace Company to restore the external forms of the extinct animals to their natural gigantic size. He devoted three and a half years to the construction of thirty-three life-size dinosaur models which were placed in the Crystal Palace Park. Following this, Hawkins came to New York in 1868, lectured on popular science in the hall of the Cooper Union and began to assemble a new menagerie of sculptured dinosaurs. At that time, Central Park was being landscaped under the direction of Frederick Law Olmstead. Unfortunately, in 1871, before either the park or the dinosaurs were finished, New York City politics intervened. The corrupt Tammany Hall-Boss Tweed machine took control of city politics, and Hawkins's dinosaurs were destroyed. Sadly, those dinosaur models were broken up and buried in the south end of the park, never to be found. Hawkins left New York an embittered man. That same year, the Tweed administration asked Jacob Wrey Mould to design temporary structures for the Menagerie on the Arsenal grounds. By November 1871, a deer house had already been completed, but Olmsted and Vaux ordered it to be demolished.

Another important cultural phenomenon associated with the Central Park Menagerie is the influence of Charles Darwin's theories of human evolution. Late nineteenth century visitors were both drawn to and repulsed by monkeys. Pete, on the other hand, would not be aware of Darwin and his response to the monkey is one of great admiration, based on his observation of the monkey's hostility. "Once at the Menagerie he went into a trance of admiration before the spectacle of a very small monkey threatening to trash a cageful because one of them had pulled his tail."

Incorporated in the year of Crane's birth, the Metropolitan Museum of Art is another venue which Pete and Maggie visit. "Dese little jugs" about which Pete explodes were part of the Cesnola Collection of Cypriote Antiquities, at that time the largest and most famous collection of its kind in the world. The exhibit included sculptures, bronzes, vases, terracottas, gems, glass, and jewelry from Cyprus dating from ca. 2500 B.C. to ca. A.D. 300. Acquired by Luigi Palma di Cesnola (1832–1904), a Civil War veteran and American diplomat in Cyprus, the collection was purchased by the newly formed Metropolitan Museum between 1874 and 1876. The reference probably would have been understood by a contemporary reader of the novel. And, since admission to both the Zoo and the Museum was free on Sundays, the contemporary reader would also have recognized that Pete was not being extravagant in taking Maggie to this popular uptown museum.

Works Cited

Davis, Linda H. *Badge of Courage: The Life of Stephen Crane.* Boston and New York: Houghton Mifflin Company (1998): 56–57.

Harlow, Alvin F. *Old Bowery Days: The Chronicles of a Famous Street.* New York and London: D. Appleton & Company (1931): 407.

McNamara, Brooks. *The New York Concert Saloon: "The Devil's Own Nights."* Cambridge: Cambridge University Press (2002): 102.

Dennett, Andrea Stulman. *Weird and Wonderful: The Dime Museum in America.* New York and London: New York University Press (1997): 58.

List of Characters

Maggie Johnson, the title character, is a young woman who grows up in the squalor and poverty of the Bowery in New York City's Lower East Side. While her mother, Mary, is an abusive alcoholic and her brother, Jimmie, is a brute, Maggie manages to grow up a beautiful young woman with the hope and desire for a better way of life. Maggie's downfall, however, occurs as the result of her love for Pete, a young man who appears to be confident and sophisticated, but who nevertheless abandons her. As a result of that abandonment, Maggie becomes a prostitute in order to earn a living, which further causes her to become the object of scandalous talk in the neighborhood. In the end, Maggie succumbs to her terrible environment and lifestyle, but the reason she dies is very unclear—she may have been a murder victim or, possibly, taken her own life. Nevertheless, Crane's message is very clear— Maggie is the victim of the poverty she is born into and, most tragically, cannot escape.

Jimmie is Maggie's brother and Mary's son. Jimmie, the first character we hear about, is in the midst of a street battle. He is violent and devoid of compassion for the other children. He also lacks the ability to understand his own combative behavior. Having seduced and abandoned women he is guilty of the same abusive treatment as Maggie's seducer, Pete. Nevertheless, Jimmie hates Pete for what he has done to Maggie, while never recognizing that he has behaved the same way. Ironically, instead of having sympathy for Maggie, Jimmie blames his sister for causing the scandal. Though he has acquired the brutish characteristics necessary of the urban poverty which has molded his personality, Jimmie's survival is simply that and nothing more.

Mary is Maggie and Jimmie's mother. She is an abusive and vicious alcoholic, who is given over to uncontrollable outrage, spending much of her time destroying her physical environment. Her rage is so terrifying that Maggie runs away. Indeed, she is even the butt of joke within her own rough neighborhood. Nevertheless, Mary Johnson also has the audacity to criticize Maggie's behavior as immoral. She is also extremely manipulative as evidenced by her staging a scene of mourning for the daughter whom she never loved.

Pete is a friend of Jimmie Johnson and a very affected bartender. As a result of his talk about money and his pretense to offer a better way of life, he succeeds in seducing the innocent Maggie Johnson. However, he soon loses interest in Maggie when his attention is turned to an equally pretentious and manipulative woman named Nellie. As it turns out, Nellie has no love for Peter, but has merely been using him for his money.

Tommie, Maggie's youngest brother, dies early in the novel, a victim of his pernicious environment.

Father of Maggie, Jimmie and Tommie, and husband of Mary. He is an alcoholic and casually abusive towards his children. He even resorts to stealing beer from Jimmie. The father dies early in the novel and Crane only gives him a last name.

The old woman has no name. She lives in the same tenement house as the Johnson family and befriends the Johnson children. She even offers Maggie shelter after the young woman has been shunned by her own abusive mother.

Miss Smith has only a brief appearance in the last scene of the novel. She encourages Mary Johnson into her false sentimental act of mourning for her deceased daughter Maggie.

Billie is a violent little Rum Alley child. He first appears at the beginning of the narrative where he is in embroiled in a street fight with Jimmie. Billie acquires the same violent behavior as Jimmie and becomes Jimmie's ally in his hatred towards Pete.

Summary and Analysis

Maggie opens with a street battle between rival gangs in the impoverished Bowery. Nothing less than the "honor of Rum Alley" is at stake, lead by Maggie's brother, Jimmie Johnson. A small boy, "livid with fury, Jimmie hurls invectives against the Devil's Row mob. The scene is at once interminably violent and blindly savage. "On their small, convulsed faces there shone the grins of true assassins." When Jimmie finally ends up at the bottom of a pile of attackers, it is the angry and arrogant Pete, "with an air of challenge over his eye," who comes to his rescue. "Between his teeth, a cigar stump was tilted at the angle of defiance." But his "rescue" notwithstanding, Jimmie is soon embroiled in a far worse struggle when his abusive father arrives on the scene, only to bring him home to an equally destructive domestic situation. In the larger context of this novel, it is simply not possible to be rescued from the devastating effects of urban poverty in New York's Lower East Side.

When Jimmie and his father return home (**Chapter 2**), we enter the terrify world of the Lower East Side tenement, "a dark region where, from a careening building, a dozen gruesome doorways gave up loads of babies to the street and gutter." The return home is anything but a place of safe haven but, rather, a world of interminable fighting and swearing and physical violence. Indeed, "gruesome" is an oft-repeated word for Stephen Crane expressing both the horror and the inhumane conditions of life in the Bowery slums. As soon as he enters his tenement, a structure which itself is threatened by "the weight of humanity stamping about its bowels," the relentlessly combative Jimmie gets into a fight with his sister Maggie. She is concerned about their mother's violent reaction to Jimmie's street fighting, a response that is habitual due to Mary Johnson's alcoholism. And, shortly thereafter, as Jimmie walks into the room, his alcoholic mother immediately flies into a rage. Her "massive shoulders heaved with anger.... She dragged him to an unholy sink, and, soaking a rag in water, began to scrub his lacerated face with it," followed by her banishing the father from their flat. Not surprisingly, the father likewise seeks to escape the "living hell" through alcohol, "determined upon a vengeful drunk," while the terrified children passively retreat from this brutal exchange.

Following his father's departure, "[t]he little boy ran to the halls, shrieking like a monk in an earthquake." And, though the frightened Jimmie is offered some temporary sanctuary by an elderly neighbor, "a gnarled and leathery personage who could don, at will, an expression of great virtue," there is scant reason to have any faith or credence from such a person. The old woman is part of the brutal reality of the slums (**Chapter 3**) with a criminal history of her own. "Once, when a lady had dropped her purse on the sidewalk, the gnarled woman grabbed it and smuggled it with great dexterity beneath her cloak." Indeed, Crane is making a strong statement that slum life offers no hope of escape and that this environment is devoid of any spiritual relief. And to compound both our distrust and lack of confidence in her ability to shelter a child, she sends Jimmie on a dangerous mission to buy her some beer from a saloon where, not surprisingly, he is soon assailed by his own father, a "lurching figure" set within a "gruesome doorway." His father wants nothing more than to steal the beer from his young son. "The father wrenched the pail from the urchin.... There was a tremendous gulping movement and the beer was gone." When Jimmie finally returns home, both parents are drunk, exchanging "howls and curses, groans and shrieks, confusingly in chorus as if a battle were raging." Indeed, life in the slums is an unending tragedy, and the use of the word chorus here could even be can seen as analogous to the chorus in a Greek tragedy which had the function of both participating in and commenting on the events taking place. Further, Crane is also implying that the reality of the slums resembles life in a jungle in that the abject fright in which the children are forced to live makes them akin to animals who must hide in fear of those who seek to devour them. In her mother's presence, Maggie is seen eating "like a small pursued tigress," and both she and her brother are huddled in abject fright, "crouched until the ghost-mists of dawn appeared at the window."

After the passage of some considerable, but unspecified time, we learn that both the unremarkable father and his infant son, Tommie, have died for some vague reason (**Chapter 4**). Their demise is reported in a tragically deadpan and unremarkable style and, thus, their presence quickly and tragically evaporates from both the world of the tenement and the consciousness of the reader. "The babe, Tommie died. He went away in a white, insignificant coffin." During this time, Jimmie continues to grow up into a brooding young man, "sullen with thoughts of a hopeless attitude where grew fruit," that the sum total of his life experiences had presaged, a downtrodden human being gainsaid whatever happiness he perceives more fortunate men to enjoy. Chapter 4 provides a glimpse of the consequences of a deteriorating character when Jimmie takes a job as a teamster driving horses through lower Manhattan, scouting trouble wherever it exists and readily becoming embroiled in any available ruckus. "In revenge, he resolved never to move out of the way of anything, until formidable circumstances ... forced him to it." Indeed, this job makes Jimmie even more belligerent and alienated, so much so that he shuns all religion and faith. Devoid of all hope of a better way of life, Jimmie is spiritually lost, "for he himself could perceive that Providence had caused it clearly to be written." And, as seen in a multitude of instances in *Maggie* wherein Crane uses animal analogues to describe his characters' emotional responses, Jimmie's awe-stricken reverence towards the world of mechanical objects, which he cannot overpower with brute force, is likened to the response of a dog. "A fire engine was enshrined in his heart as an appalling thing that he loved with a distant dog-like devoting."

Parallel to Jimmie's growing into bitter manhood, Maggie, who "blossom[s] in a mud puddle," by way of contrast, manages to nurture and retain a certain beauty despite the ravages of the Bowery and the filth of Rum Alley in **Chapter 5.** "She grew to be a most rare and wonderful production of a tenement district." When she does go to work in a sweatshop which manufactures collars and cuffs, "the name of whose brand could be noted for its irrelevancy to anything in connection with collars," Crane emphasizes the extent to which the working poor are met with the same loss of identity they have known since childhood. All the shop-girls are of "various shades of yellow discontent." But the most tragic, and ultimately fatal, consequence of poverty is Maggie's vulnerability to the advances of the boastful Pete, with whom she becomes infatuated—a young man whose "patent-leather shoes looked like murder-fitted weapons." "There was valor and contempt for circumstances in the glance of his eye. He waved his hands like a man of the world, who dismisses religion and philosophy." As a result of her encounter with Pete, Maggie will continue to spiral down towards her own destruction, a fate that unfolds in a series of erroneous and misguided readings of other people's characters and true motives. Maggie is equally susceptible to the same gullible adoration when Pete regales her with his tall tales of strength and manliness on the job, telling would-be troublemakers to "get deh hell outa here," and, most audaciously, of appreciation and commendation from his boss. "But deh boss ... he says, 'Pete, yes done jes' right!'" The sweet and innocent Maggie has no way of discerning Pete's dishonesty and false bravado and, sadly, falls prey to his empty promise of false hope because she is still able to imagine in Pete the possibility of escaping the poverty and degradation into which she has been born. "Maggie perceived that here was the beau ideal of a man.... Under the trees of her dream-gardens there had always walked a lover."

Chapter 6 marks the beginning of Maggie's seduction into Pete's very sinister plan. For his part, Pete wastes no time or words in snaring her into his evil web. "'Say, Mag, I'm stuck on yer shape. It's outa sight." And Maggie, for her part, is completely enchanted with Pete and what she perceives to be his exalted status in the world. "Maggie marveled at him and surrounded him with greatness." Maggie longs to bring beauty into her depressed surroundings, a world of "hardship and insults," and expends a great deal of effort and money to improve the bleak atmosphere of home, a "flowered cretonne for a lambrequin," a decorative drapery usually hung from the edge of a shelf or above a window. But, alas, Maggie's drunken mother, with a propensity for destroying furniture, will not allow any hope or beauty in her life. "She had vented some phase of drunken fury upon the lambrequin. It lay in a bedraggled heap in the corner.... The knots of blue ribbons appeared like violated flowers." And, the notion of transgression in the "courtship" of Pete and naïve Maggie is thereby presaged.

Shortly after Maggie begins to go out with Pete he introduces her to the seedy forms of entertainment available in the slums (**Chapter 7**). In his attempt to impress the very naïve Maggie, their first date is at a beer-garden, "a great green-hued hall," whose clientele is comprised of factory workers and manual laborers, "people who showed that all day they strove with their hands." In an effort to enhance the aura and illusion of gentility, Pete appears chivalrous in Maggie's eyes, "display[ing] the consideration of a cultured gentleman who knew what was due," in order to lure her into his deceitful trap, and he succeeds. His deceptive ways works like a charm on Maggie. "Her heart warmed as she reflected upon his condescension."

Typical of the concert halls of the time, there is a female singer accompanied by an orchestra, in this instance a girl bedecked in "pink dress with short skirts, [who] galloped upon the stage" before the leering gaze of tipsy men, who occasionally tried to touch her. The girl's response is mechanical—from the ten-minute smile she bestows upon the audience to the finale in which she dons "some of those grotesque attitudes which were at the time popular" in the more posh up-town theatres, creating yet another illusion of respectability for the denizens of the slums. But, perhaps the most poignant aspect of this world of illusion and false promise is Maggie's innocent willingness to be persuaded that she can escape the life she is born to. Though thoughts of the sweatshop have receded from her consciousness, she does not understand that in reality she has merely exchanged one mechanical world for another. From the tawdry bill of available entertainments in a place like Rum Alley. Maggie now becomes unquestioningly obedient as Pete silently claims ownership of her life. Their first date concludes late at night in front of a "gruesome doorway."

The immediate effect of Maggie's association with Pete is a growing discontent with her own life and a feeling of superiority over the other girls in the sweatshop, still unaware that her romantic fantasies of Pete and the life she imagines him living are all a fiction (**Chapter 8**). "She wondered as she regarded some of the grizzled women in the room, mere mechanical contrivances sewing seams and grinding out ... tales of imagined or real girlhood happiness." Nevertheless, Maggie also becomes painfully aware of the fleeting nature of her youthful beauty, resulting in a realization of the value of "the bloom upon her cheeks." Though she does not yet know that Pete has an agenda, she is now cognizant that her good looks are worth something. And this new consciousness manifests itself in an increasing exaltation of Pete, who "loomed like a golden sun to Maggie," in contrast to the bleak cityscape of life in the Bowery slums.

However, when Maggie's thoughts turn to a Sunday afternoon outing with Pete, Crane introduces a notable irony. While Maggie is duped by Pete's deceptive air of sophistication, she nevertheless exhibits a remarkable degree of imagination which Pete utterly lacks. His focus is merely to exploit Maggie and, accordingly, is simply exhibiting meaningless gestures of gallantry in his effort to ensnare her. He has difficulty planning a respectable date for a Sunday afternoon with Maggie until he remembers the various distractions of Central Park, which include the Menagerie and the Museum of Arts. Within the context of his very narrow focus on life as a continuous exploitation of others, Pete has very little interest in these entertainments, except for one telling detail, his fascination with the monkeys. "Once at the Menagerie he went into a trance of admiration before the spectacle of a very small monkey threatening to trash a cageful because one of them had pulled his tail." It is hardly surprising that Pete would become interested in this creature known for its ability to imitate man and for its belligerence in this particular instance. His reaction to the Museum of Art is much different as he is not at all interested in ancient artifacts. "'Look at all dese little jugs! ... What deh blazes use is dem?'"

Later on, when Maggie and Pete are together on weekday evenings, they attend the conventional melodramatic plays so popular in the 1890s Bowery. In fact, Stephen Crane had a low opinion of these melodrama performances with their elaborate crises and overblown emotional displays in which a "brain-clutching heroine [is] rescued from the palatial home of her guardian." Maggie, on the other hand, is completely given over to sympathy for these exaggerated characters and plots. "To Maggie and the rest of the audience, this was transcendental realism." Tragically, she is laboring under the blind-sighted belief that she will be able to escape her poverty. "She rejoiced at the way in which the poor and virtuous eventually surmounted the wealthy and wicked."

In **Chapter 9** the scene shifts to a group of violent urchins outside a saloon with the figure of an old woman yelling at them from "the frame of a gruesome doorway." To further emphasize the repulsive nature of slum life, one night Pete comes to call on Maggie, only to observe her drunken mother and enraged brother embroiled in a violent argument. At this point, Mary launches into a vituperative denunciation against her daughter Maggie, telling her to "[g]o the hell an' good riddance." In her perceptive understanding of Pete's true motives, Mary Johnson assumes that Pete has already ruined her daughter. "'Yer a disgrace to yer people, damn ye. An' now, git out an' go ahn wid dat doe-faced jude of yours.'" Ironically, with this abusive dismissal, the requisite conditions are set for Maggie to leave with Pete, which now will surely lead to her seduction and final downfall. As for Maggie's brother Jimmie, we are told that he has only a vague notion that it is wrong for a friend to come to another friend's home with the purpose of ruining the sister.

On the following evening, Jimmie listens to one of his begrimed and elderly neighbors, who desperately wants to recount what she has observed after Mary consigned Maggie to the devil in **Chapter 10**. Apparently, the old woman saw Maggie crying and heard her ask Pete if he loved her. "'It was deh funnies' t'ing I ever saw,' she cried, coming close to him and leering." That this leathery old woman finds humor in Maggie's desperate need to be reassured that she has not been utterly ruined tragically underscores a fundamental lack of humanity and compassion for Maggie's plight by those who are made to suffer the same daily degradation. Needless to say, Mary Johnson is equally blind to see the harm she has visited upon her sweet and unsuspecting daughter when she heaps blame on her sweet and unsuspecting daughter and, for that matter, her failure as a parent.

Chapter 11 begins with a lurid description of nighttime in the Bowery. "The open mouth of a saloon called seductively to passengers to enter and annihilate sorrow or create rage." This statement is evocative and frightening in the image it evokes of an animated material world aiding and abetting the inevitable corruption which it has witnessed. Inside this establishment, where "an odor of grasping, begrimed hands and munching mouths pervaded," Pete, dressed in a white jacket, is working as bartender. Jimmie and his companion, Billie, enter drunk, with the intention of provoking a violent confrontation. In no time at all, a fight ensues as Jimmie's grimy partner begins to make derogatory comments about Pete. The scene rapidly takes on the character of jungle warfare. Pete assumes the "glare of a panther," and soon "[t]he three frothing creatures on the floor buried themselves in a frenzy for blood." The end result is that Jimmie, narrowly escapes the approaching policeman, while Billie and Pete are arrested. Once again, the curse of the Bowery is implicit in Jimmie's efforts to avoid arrest—namely that he is forever condemned to the brutal life of poverty.

A short time later, Pete and Maggie are at a very disreputable bar, "a hall of irregular shape," with Maggie now completely and tragically dependent on the disreputable Pete (**Chapter 12**). Much to her detriment, Maggie still sees Pete as her savior, with "wealth and prosperity in his clothes," and the all but realized promise of a better way of life. "She thought of her former Rum Alley environment and turned to regard Pete's strong protecting fists.... She imagined a future rose-tinted...." Needless to say, Maggie does not consider herself degraded or in any way diminished by Pete but, rather, safe from all harm. "She would be disturbed by no apprehensions, so long as Pete adored her as he now said he did." Indeed, so oblivious is she to her tawdry surroundings that she recognizes neither the impending danger of other men's stares nor Pete's pivotal role in bringing her to destruction. "At times men at other tables regarded the girl furtively. Pete, aware of it, nodded at her and grinned. He felt proud."

In **Chapter 13**, the story shifts to Jimmie who, we are told, stayed away from home for several days following the scuffle at the saloon, lest he be caught. His irresponsible mother, on the other hand, wastes no time in casting blame and aspersion on Mary. "May Gawd curse her forever.... May she eat nothin' but stones and deh dirt in deh street." It is also important to note that Mary Johnson considers herself a good mother who brought her daughter up well. "'When a girl is bringed up deh way I bringed up Maggie, how kin sh go the deh devil?'" Once again, Crane's recurring implication is that those who are uneducated and forced to live in daily degradation do not have the ability to understand how they are caught in a vicious and self-perpetuating cycle that is passed on from one generation to the next. Finally, Maggie's mother is equally adept at manipulating situations to her own advantage and does not hesitate to implicate Maggie for her own uncontrollable drunken rage when confronted by the police. The police finally catch on, observing that in her numerous prior arrests she had the same excuse, a curious fact that produced a record of her having forty-two daughters in all.

For his part, Jimmie spends a fleeting moment wondering whether "all sisters, excepting his own, could advisedly be ruined," and, just as easily, forgets this thought. There is also a self-serving aspect in Jimmie's dismissal of Maggie's plight, for he is just as guilty as Pete. "[H]e wondered vaguely if some of the women of his acquaintance had brothers. Nevertheless, his mind did not for an instant confuse himself with those brothers, nor his sister with theirs." There is some faint suggestion that Jimmie has the ability to achieve a true and more compassionate consciousness about Maggie's fate, but sadly these thoughts are quickly brushed aside and never shared with anyone else. "[H]e, once, almost came to a conclusion that his sister would have been more firmly good had she better known why. However, he felt that he could not hold such a view. He threw it aside hastily."

In **Chapter 14**, the scene shifts to another concert saloon, "a hilarious hall" with a group of unctuous men. Here, "soiled waiters" are seen "swooping down like hawks" amidst walls covered over with "dusty monstrosities." Maggie has now been living with Pete for three weeks, during which time "her spaniel-like dependence had been magnified." Shortly after their arrival, a woman, named Nell, enters the saloon with a young boy, who appears to be her date. And Pete will soon show his true nature as he is easily seduced by a former acquaintance. As soon as he sees her, he becomes very anxious to speak with her. For her part, Maggie gazes upon this unfamiliar woman with an extremely misguided awe and admiration, as she believes Nell to be "a woman of brilliance and audacity." Nevertheless, Maggie's misjudgment notwithstanding, the reader soon finds out that Nell has no scruples and is only interested in money. Having just returned to town, Nell is disappointed about a business venture, which she explains to Pete. "'Well he didn't have as many stamps [slang for money] as he tried to make out, so I shook him, that's all.'" Pete becomes increasingly preoccupied with Nell, insisting that he needs to explain why he previously stood her up. Pete and Nell walk outside and Maggie is left with the young man named Freddie, although he protests that isn't his real name. The chapter closes with Maggie having been abandoned by Pete, while Freddie helps her onto a street car, paying her fare, and "leer[ing] kindly at her through the rear window."

Chapter 15 relates the details of Maggie's return home, the terrible treatment she receives from her mother and her banishment from the Johnson home. In her dreary walk home,

Maggie is portrayed in terms of her abject misery and lack of hope. Indeed, in the first three paragraphs, Crane describes her as "a forlorn woman." When she reaches her mother's house, Mrs. Johnson goes into one of her familiar rages, insulting and ridiculing Maggie in front of her brother Jimmie, "like a glib showman at a museum," while Maggie becomes increasingly alienated. "She edged about as if unable to find a place on the floor to put her feet." In truth, Maggie is homeless and when she leaves, it will be for the last time. Shunned by all the neighbors except an old woman who offers her a place to stay, Maggie has no choice but to leave as an exile. Moreover, similar to Maggie's tragic abandonment and homelessness wrought by Pete's shameful exploitation of her, Chapter 15 offers a parallel story of Jimmie's abusive behavior towards women. In another portentous scene we are introduced to an equally forsaken woman wandering the streets alone at night. This woman turns out to be Hattie, a woman whom Jimmie had likewise rejected. "The forlorn woman had a peculiar face.... as if some one had sketched with cruel forefinger indelible lines about her mouth." Sadly, Hattie's chance encounter with Jimmie on this particular evening ends with her errant lover summarily dismissing her once again. "'Say, fer Gawd's sake, Hattie, don't foller me from one end of deh city the deh odder.... Go chase yerself, fer Gawd's sake.'"

Ironically, **Chapter 16** begins with Crane telling the reader that Pete has no clue that he is responsible for Maggie's spiraling downfall. He "did not consider that he had ruined Maggie. If he had a thought that her soul could never smile again, he would have believed the mother and brother ... responsible for it." But his blind-sighted dismissal of Maggie's tragic predicament is met with a similar response from Nell, who "showed a disposition to ridicule him," while Pete very foolishly protests that he never cared very much for Maggie. Nell responds by laughing at him, for she has no love for him. Nevertheless, Pete only senses that his taste in women is being criticized and thus he continues to remonstrate, in vain to the disinterested woman of brilliance and audacity. A short time later, Pete is back at work behind the bar, fully conscious of the need to present a professional and proprietary demeanor, when he spots Maggie walking past and becomes agitated. In his irritated response to Maggie, Pete demonstrates that his only concern is for the air of respectability he feels compelled to maintain for the saloon. "'What deh hell deh yeh wanna tag aroun' atter me fer? Yeh'll git me in the trouble wid deh ol' man ...'" Pete makes it clear that he will assume no responsibility and Maggie is forced to accept his response. And, in a final comment on institutional failure, Crane makes it clear that the Church has reneged on its spiritual responsibilities when Maggie encounters a clergyman who similarly shuns her. "[H]e gave a convulsive movement and saved his respectability by a vigorous side-step. He did not risk it to save a soul." With this last dismissal, Maggie's terrible fate is now inevitable. It is hardly surprising that she would fall into a life of prostitution, "a girl of the painted cohorts of the city."

Chapter 17 continues Maggie's tragic story several months later on a rainy evening, amidst "the gloomy districts near the river, where the tall black factories shut in the street." Various men, "wet wanderers," make disinterested comments to her, quickly explaining why they are unable to engage her services. Finally, Maggie is accosted by a huge fat man in greasy clothes. As he begins to follow, the reader is left to imagine the outcome of this sad encounter as we lose sight of their destination. The scene is dark and foreboding. "At their feet the river appeared a deathly black hue."

In **Chapter 18** the scene returns to a very drunk Pete, sitting in a secluded section of the saloon, cavorting with several giggling women who "nod their heads approvingly" at him. One of these silly women is Nell. They are all only interested in his buying them drinks. During his long and intoxicated protestation of benign goodwill Pete will eventually collapse. However, before this calamity befalls, Pete, "[o]verwhelmed by a spasm of drunken adoration," gives Nell money while making an empty declaration of his love for her, to which act of kindness Nell responds by calling him "a damn fool."

Chapter 19 begins with Jimmie delivering the terrible news of Maggie's fate in a pathetically brief and deadpan announcement, equally as dismissive as the description of the death of Tommie in Chapter 4. "A soiled, unshaven man pushed open the door and entered. "'Well,'" said he, 'Mag's dead.'" In response to this tragic news, Mary Johnson, who has been "eating like a fat monk in a picture," launches into a highly melodramatic and wholly unconvincing act of uncontrollable grief and mourning. In a word, Maggie's mother makes a complete spectacle of herself. "The neighbors began to gather in the hall, staring in at the weeping woman as if watching the contortions of a dying dog." And her feigned forgiveness of her daughter, her "disobed'ent chil," is equally as empty. In a story in which the survivors are utterly and absolutely unable to extricate themselves from the impoverished world of the Lower East Side, an early death is Maggie's only means of escape. With the encouragement of the attendant mourners who now believe that Maggie's sins will be judged by a higher authority, Mary Johnson finally decides to forgive her daughter, when it no longer matters.

Critical Views

MICHAEL ROBERTSON ON CRANE'S
JOURNALISTIC EXPERIENCE

Building on the perceptions of *Maggie*'s first readers, later critics assumed that a simple three-step process lay behind Crane's New York City writing: Crane observed New York's slums, wrote about what he saw in the newspaper, then used his newspaper sketches as raw material for his slum novels, *Maggie* and *George's Mother* (1896). As Tom Wolfe put it, Crane's Bowery sketches were "warm-ups for novels."[8] However, the relation between Crane's New York City journalism and fiction is not so simple as has been assumed. Both biographical investigation and literary analysis complicate any attempt to construct a genealogy for *Maggie* that moves from observation to journalism to fiction.

Although doubt has been cast on claims by Crane's fraternity brothers at Syracuse University that he wrote *Maggie* as a nineteen-year-old freshman in the spring of 1891, it seems certain that Crane completed a draft of the novel before he moved to New York City in the fall of 1892.[9] When Crane started *Maggie*, his knowledge of New York's mean streets was based on his teenaged excursions into the city from relatives' homes in New Jersey. All of Crane's New York City newspaper sketches followed his drafting of the novel, confounding any attempt to regard the journalism as a warm-up for *Maggie*.

Frank Norris, who was working as a journalist in San Francisco when *Maggie* appeared, was the first writer to call into question the notion that *Maggie* records Crane's observations in the slums of New York. Norris wrote perceptively in his review of the novel that Crane was drawing on a long tradition of slum literature: "Most of his characters are old acquaintances in the world of fiction.... In ordinary hands the tale of 'Maggie' would be 'twice told.'"[10] Subsequent scholars have identified the novel's debt not only to the world of fiction but also to the mass of nonfiction writing on the evils

39

of slum life produced by reformers and clergy.[11] Crane's deeply religious family would have been familiar with the works of crusading Christian reformers like Charles Loring Brace and the Reverend Thomas DeWitt Talmage, both of whom wrote copiously about the problems of lower New York during the 1870s and 1880s, when Crane was growing up. In the early 1890s secular reformers such as Benjamin O. Flower and writers for his magazine, the *Arena*—where Crane later published—frequently railed against the slums.

Its plot and characters inherited from dozens of stories and sermons, *Maggie* can scarcely be identified as journalistic—or even, despite the many readers who have pinned the label on it, as realistic. Crane contributed to the confusion about his novel when he inscribed in several copies of the first edition, "[*Maggie*] tries to show that environment is a tremendous thing in the world and frequently shapes lives regardless."[12] The inscription implies that *Maggie* is a naturalistic text, a rigorous investigation into the effects of the New York City slums on their inhabitants. However, as D.H. Lawrence reminded students of American literature, one must trust the tale, not the teller.[13] Crane's title character seems virtually unaffected by her environment. She is, in the text's melodramatic phrase, a flower who "blossomed in a mud puddle," an icon of purity placed, improbably, in a monstrous family with a mother and father who regularly attack each other in alcoholic rages, smashing enough furniture over the course of the novel to fill a warehouse.[14] Crane's story of a poor and innocent virgin seduced and then driven into a life of prostitution fits snugly into the conventions of Victorian melodrama.

Maggie owes nothing directly to Crane's New York City newspaper sketches, which he wrote after drafting the novel. However, this is not to say that Crane's first novel has nothing in common with his journalism. *Maggie* reflects the same thematic and stylistic preoccupations evident in Crane's early newspaper writing about Sullivan County and the New Jersey shore. The early journalism and *Maggie* show three major continuities. First, *Maggie*, like the shore reports, is notable for its lack of overt moralistic commentary. Just as Crane's

New-York Tribune articles avoid the tongue clucking about overly daring bathing suits or backroom gambling that was common in resort news, *Maggie* lacks the condemnations of drink, violence, and sexual misconduct that were standard in slum literature. Next, *Maggie* is remarkable for its irony; as Thomas Beer remarked, it is the first entirely ironic novel written by an American.[15] Maggie's drunken mother, who envisions herself as an excellent parent and a pious Christian; her truck-driving brother, who "menaced mankind" from street corners (20); her lover, an arrogant dandy—all are treated with the sharp-eyed irony that Crane used to describe middle-class vacationers at the New Jersey shore. Finally, the prose of *Maggie*, like that of Crane's early journalism, is strikingly fresh and original. A number of elements contribute to the distinctiveness of Crane's style in these early works. His writing abounds in startling figures of speech that evoke sharp images in readers' minds and, at the same time, move beyond the referents and draw attention to themselves as linguistic constructions. For example, in both Crane's journalism and in *Maggie* buildings become disconcertingly animate: a *Tribune* article describes a "palpitat[ing]" auditorium and tents that "rear their white heads under the trees,"[16] whereas a description of a slum in *Maggie* tells how "from a careening building, a dozen gruesome doorways gave up loads of babies to the street and the gutter" (11). Such deliberately disorienting descriptions follow one another in quick succession in Crane's work, joined by syntactically jerky sentences that are in turn assembled into short disconnected paragraphs. This abrupt style was a journalistic convention of the era. Shore reports got their unity from their setting rather than from a sustained narrative, and New Jersey Coast News Bureau reports commonly contained a half-dozen unconnected news items. However, the disconnected style that was conventional in a newspaper context appears radically new in *Maggie*.

Maggie is indeed related to Crane's early journalism, but the relation is more complex than early reviewers suggested. The myth of the reporter-artist implies a simple progression from observation to journalism to fiction. In addition, the myth places fiction at the top of an immutable literary hierarchy, with journalism below, serving as a stepping-stone to higher things. Critics of Stephen Crane's journalism have reinforced this hierarchical view. One of the first critics to examine Crane's newspaper journalism wrote of the inevitable conflict between "reportage and serious fiction" and concluded that the principal benefit of Crane's newspaper experience was to strengthen and sharpen his talent for "more serious creative work."[17] A more recent critic wrote approvingly of Crane's effort "to seek out the higher truths of fiction, beyond the bare facts of journalism."[18]

Notes

8. Tom Wolfe, *The New Journalism* (New York: Harper & Row, 1973), 45.

9. James B. Colvert, "Introduction," *Bowery Tales*, vol. 1 of *The Works of Stephen Crane*, ed. Fredson Bowers (Charlottesville: University Press of Virginia, 1969), xxxiii–xxxvii; Stanley Wertheim and Paul Sorrentino, *The Crane Log: A Documentary Life of Stephen Crane, 1871–1900* (New York: G. K. Hall, 1994), 62, 80.

10. Donald Pizer, ed., *Literary Criticism of Frank Norris* (Austin: University of Texas Press, 1964), 164.

11. James B. Colvert, *Stephen Crane* (New York: Harcourt Brace Jovanovich, 1984), 47–50; Marcus Cunliffe, "Stephen Crane and the American Background of *Maggie*," *American Quarterly* 7 (1955): 31–114; Laura Hapke, *Girls Who Went Wrong: Prostitutes in American Fiction, 1885–1917* (Bowling Green, Ohio: Bowling Green State University Popular Press, 1989), 45–67; Giorgio Mariani, *Spectacular Narratives: Representations of Class and War in Stephen Crane and the American 1890s* (New York: Peter Lang, 1992), 35–67.

12. Stanley Wertheim and Paul Sorrentino, eds., *The Correspondence of Stephen Crane*, vol. 1 (New York: Columbia University Press, 1988), 52–53.

13. D.H. Lawrence, *Studies in Classic American Literature* (1923; New York: Penguin, 1977), 8.

14. Stephen Crane, *Maggie: A Girl of the Streets (A Story of New York)* (1893), in *Stephen Crane: Poetry and Prose* (New York: Library of America, 1984), 24. Subsequent quotations are cited parenthetically.

15. Thomas Beer, *Stephen Crane: A Study in American Letters* (New York: Knopf, 1924), 85.

16. [Stephen Crane] "Meetings Begun at Ocean Grove," *New-York Tribune*, July 2, 1892, p. 4.

17. Joseph J. Kwiat, "The Newspaper Experience: Crane, Norris, and Dreiser," *Nineteenth-Century Fiction* 8 (1953): 103, 117.

18. Thomas A. Gullason, "The 'Lost' Newspaper Writings of Stephen Crane," *Syracuse University Library Associates Courier* 21 (1986): 68.

DONALD PIZER ON THE RELATIONSHIP OF BREVITY TO NATURALISM

Maggie was of course neglected on its initial publication in 1893, but since its reissue in 1896, and especially since the rediscovery of Crane and his work in the early 1920s, it has attracted a great deal of attention. One source of interest in the novel lies in its benchmark role as Crane's first major work of fiction. In what ways, it can be asked, did Crane's ideas and techniques change—or, to use the old-fashioned term, develop—from their first significant representation in *Maggie* through *The Red Badge of Courage* and into the major stories of 1896 to 1898? Another major critical role of *Maggie* has been in its character as the first self-conscious expression of literary naturalism in America and therefore as a novel which appears to offer an initial working definition of this important tendency in American fiction. And yet another critical concern has been the ways in which the startling stylistics of the work presage many of the devices which are considered central to American literary modernism.[1]

Of these three major approaches to *Maggie*, it is perhaps Crane's putative naturalism which has received the most attention. The story of a girl of the slums from an alcoholic family who is first seduced and then drawn into prostitution and suicide speaks to the origin of naturalism in the late nineteenth-century desire to create a fiction which illustrates the workings of natural law—that is, the forces of heredity and environment—in human affairs. Of course, it is the distinctive nature of Crane's acceptance in *Maggie* of a naturalistic credo which has principally engaged critics of the novel and of

43

Crane's career in general. Crane's notion of environment, it is now widely believed, extends beyond the animality and prison-like social conditions of slum life to include the non-functional and thus destructive ideas and values of slum dwellers. In addition, Crane's irony in the novel, it is now realized, extends the intent of naturalism beyond the demonstration of natural law to a challenging of middle-class assumptions about the relationship of natural law to moral truth. Might not an average reader's beliefs about moral justice—about the impossibility, for example, of discovering a prostitute in heaven have little relevance to the conditions of slum life, and therefore might not, indeed, some of his other moral assumptions have little relationship to the actual conditions of experience?[2] And finally, there have been a number of efforts to modify the belief that Crane's naturalism in *Maggie* is limited to an unyielding dismissal of human agency. One effort of this kind, for example, has been my own attempt to suggest that Crane's determinism in the work does not preclude the presence of a traditional humanistic strain of belief. Thus, in the adjacent chapters in *Maggie* which introduce us to Maggie and Jimmie now grown into adulthood, we are presented with two poignant moments in which souls seek to cry out through the bars of the prisons of their social condition. The street-wise and hardened Jimmie, whose life consists principally of beating rival teamsters and deserting pregnant sweethearts, "nevertheless" one night exclaims at the beauty of the moon. And Maggie, imprisoned in a sweat shop and devalued in her own house, nevertheless seeks to express her association of burgeoning love with physical beauty as she hangs a new household decoration in expectation of the arrival of her suitor. Neither of these impulses from the depths of being is fully or successfully articulated by Jimmie and Maggie and neither is repeated. But Crane, in the very inarticulateness and momentariness of these moments, is expressing one of the great themes of American literary naturalism and of Dreiser in particular, that of the core of sensibility present in even the seemingly most inadequate and subjugated of men and women.[3]

(...)

Let us now return to *Maggie* and to the critical problem presented by its brevity in relation both to the naturalistic themes of the weight of the social moment and the interdependence of most lives and to the naturalistic device of authorial explanation, all of which appear firmly linked to length of fictional expression. It is Crane's unique character as a naturalist, I will now argue, not to reject these preoccupations but rather to express them by means of compactness and compression rather than through fullness. Of course, in stating this premise, I realize that I am entering as well the much-discussed area of Crane's impressionism, an authorial frame of mind and literary method which has usually implied brevity rather than length. Given this seeming immediate disjuncture between the two methods, it is not surprising that some critics refuse to accept their possible mutual presence in a single work. James Nagel, for example, devotes much energy to demonstrating that an "ideological and artistic antithesis"[6] exists between naturalism, with its belief in a deterministic and objectively realizable world, and impressionism, with its stress on experience as both fleeting and relative to individual perception. These antagonistic metaphysics and epistemologies flow, in this view, into the rival fictional devices of length derived from a surety of authorial vision and brevity related to the fragmentary and inchoate nature of a character's personal vision. Other critics, however—notably Walcutt himself, who titled his chapter on Crane "Stephen Crane: Naturalist and Impressionist," and Sergio Perosa, in a landmark essay[7]—have sought to reconcile the two, though usually within discussions of *The Red Badge of Courage* rather than of *Maggie*. And finally, a third group—Ørm Øverland is the best example[8]—have posited an uneasy and not always successful interaction in Crane's work between these two ways of rendering experience.

My own approach to the issue of Crane as naturalist or impressionist, as should be suggested by the title of this essay, is to shift the angle of inquiry from general questions about Crane's ideology and artistry to the very specific matter of the apparent contradiction between conventional naturalistic length and the brevity of a specific Crane novel which is usually held to be his most naturalistic work. I will thus be arguing on the "side" of Walcutt and Perosa, but in a way that contributes further, I hope, to the complex issue of how to describe the distinctive qualities of Crane's fiction. I will seek to demonstrate the relationship between brevity and naturalism in Crane by means of a specific passage in *Maggie*.

The paragraph-length passage occurs in Chapter I. Crane has begun the novel with a description of a vicious fight between two rival children's street gangs in which the forces of Devil's Row are proving victorious over those of Rum Alley. Jimmie is the last stalwart of Rum Alley. With torn clothing and bruised and bloody body, he is surrounded by his Devil's Row antagonists. "He crooked his left arm defensively about his head and fought with cursing fury. The little boys ran to and fro, dodging, hurling stones and swearing in barbaric trebles." There then follows the paragraph I wish to examine:

> From a window of an apartment house that upreared its form from amid squat, ignorant stables, there leaned a curious woman. Some laborers, unloading a scow at a dock at the river, paused for a moment and regarded the fight. The engineer of a passive tugboat hung lazily to a railing and watched. Over on the Island, a worm of yellow convicts came from the shadow of a grey ominous building and crawled slowly along the river's bank.[9]

The passage is an excellent example of Crane's art of compression, through various acts of stylization, of naturalistic themes and devices. First, the naturalistic stress on the social moment is tersely dramatized. If the theme of the opening section of *Maggie* is that Jimmie (and therefore Maggie as well) lives in a world of animal struggle and violence in which its residents passively accept both this condition and its inevitable consequences of pain and death, then the images of the passage render this theme precisely and compactly. Jimmie's tenement world, as represented by the curious woman, because it rests on an animal base of "squat, ignorant stables," is indifferent to the violence in its midst. Even the longshoremen and the engineer of the "passive tugboat" are so inured to the violence of the world which they function on the edge of that they are only lightly engaged by the fight. And finally Crane combines the spatial sweep of the first three images, as they take us from the tenements themselves to the river, with a temporal movement, as the last image deposits us on the island prison. Out of the "grey ominous building" which itself resembles a tenement there comes the "worm" of convicts who are the inevitable products, in time, of the animal conditions of the shore.

An entire social destiny is thus here laid out through poetic devices which are inherently compact in character. The subject matter of the origin, nature, and fate of life in a slum is rendered by a series of impressionistic images, with each new sentence serving to widen the cinematic focus and with the passage as a whole enveloped by the expressionistic and surreal images of the "squat, ignorant stables" and the "yellow worm" of convicts.[10]

The passage also expresses the naturalistic theme of man's social interdependence, though it does so, in a manner that was to become characteristic of a major stream in Crane's work, by demonstrating the consequences of a failure to accept this interdependence. Each of the figures mentioned in the first three sentences—the woman, the laborers, and the engineer—constitutes a principle of indifference and passive spectatorship in the face of the social need and catastrophe which are Jimmie's fight and the convicts on their island. The repetition of the theme is closely related to its centrality in the work as a whole. Jimmie and Maggie's mother will themselves later shift into the role of spectators as Maggie makes her own journey, in the course of the novel, from the tenement to the river. Crane in the passage is therefore rendering not only a specific characteristic of Jimmie's world and destiny but also, through his compressed yet emphatic repetition, the fate of all those whose actions implicitly deny the inevitable complicity of human interaction.

Notes

1. For an excellent annotated bibliography of *Maggie* criticism, see Patrick K. Dooley, *Stephen Crane: An Annotated Bibliography of Secondary Scholarship* (New York: G.K. Hall, 1992), pp. 119–38.

2. The reading of *Maggie* as uncompromising naturalism is most closely associated with Charles C. Walcutt, *American Literary Naturalism, a Divided Stream* (Minneapolis: Univ. of Minnesota Press, 1956), pp. 67–74, though it is frequently found elsewhere as well. I seek to extend the implications of Walcutt's comments about the environmental determinism present in slum beliefs and values in my "Stephen Crane's *Maggie* and American Naturalism," *Criticism*, 7 (1965), 168–78; rpt. *Realism and Naturalism in Nineteenth-Century American Literature* (Carbondale: Southern Illinois Univ. Press, 1966; 2nd rev. ed., 1984). Rejections of a naturalistic reading of *Maggie* usually occur in book-length studies of Crane, in which the critic interprets the work in relation to themes and techniques more fully evident in Crane's later work, such as the greater stress on personal vision in *The Red Badge of Courage* (as in James Nagel's *Stephen Crane and Literary Impressionism* [University Park: Pennsylvania State Univ. Press, 1980]) or the greater stress on personal responsibility in the major short stories of 1896–98 (as in Marston LaFrance's *A Reading of Stephen Crane* [Oxford: Oxford Univ. Press, 1971]).

3. See my "American Literary Naturalism and the Humanistic Tradition," *The Theory and Practice of American Literary Naturalism* (Carbondale: Southern Illinois Univ. Press, 1993), pp. 41–44.

6. Nagel, *Stephen Crane and Literary Impressionism*, p. 32.

7. Perosa, "Naturalism and Impressionism in Stephen Crane's Fiction," in *Stephen Crane: A Collection of Critical Essays*, ed. Maurice Bassan (Englewood Cliffs, NJ.: Prentice-Hall, 1967), pp. 80–94.

8. Øverland, "The Impressionism of Stephen Crane: A Study in Style and Technique," *Americana Norvegica*, 1 (1966), 239–85.

9. *Maggie: A Girl of the Streets*, ed. Thomas Gullason (New York: W. W. Norton, 1979), pp. 3–4.

10. For a full reading of Crane's surrealism in *Maggie*, see Sydney J. Krause, "The Surrealism of Crane's Naturalism in *Maggie*," *American Literary Realism*, 16 (Autumn 1983), 253–61.

HENRY GOLEMBA ON THE LANGUAGE OF FOOD

Pete's first words to Maggie are: "Say, Mag, I'm stuck on your shape. It's outa sight" (19). Maggie's response: "She wondered what Pete dined on" (20).[1] These two quotations encode an enormous problem for Stephen Crane's. *Maggie: A Girl of the Streets*, and it reflects a crucial anxiety for American writers in the last decades of the nineteenth century who were attempting to transform new social phenomena into literary, journalistic, and photographic constructions. Pete's words reflect the realist's worry that aesthetic aims become "stuck on shape." Realism's attempt to achieve an objective point of view risks turning its subjects into objects, transforming groups of people into statistics, changing individuals into things. More drastically, realism's technique turns reality into "tecnic," and ontology becomes nothing beyond surface. The realist's motivation, welcomed by many American writers as excitingly new, once again truly "novel," was soon perceived as extremely limiting. A style that was hoped to be transcendentally "outa sight" became merely shapes and shadows, and what you saw was what you got.

(...)

Of course, one reason realistic depictions of slum life are filled with a language of food is the sheer, raw reality of starvation. Reform writings catalogue starving children, diets of moldy bread, offal in the streets, goat carcasses that decompose over the course of weeks, and the bad food of "two-cent restaurants" (Jacob Riis, *How the Other Half Lives*, 56–58). One Victor Hugoesque Riis chapter titled "The Man with the Knife" describes how a father is driven to madness and murder by the sight of rich people feasting as he pictures "those little ones crying for bread around the cold and cheerless hearth" (263–64).[4]

Moreover, many of the reform writers of the 1890s were reverends or related to ministers and thus already had a long tradition of mingling religion, food, and reform. Crane's parents are an obvious example of the blending of religion with reform, a characteristic of the reform movement that Ann Douglas and other biographers have noted. As William James observed, food had been a natural language in both reform and religious discourse in America ever since the earliest Puritans wrote of the Old and New Testaments as the twin breasts from which we suck nourishment (12). In addition, as Steven Mailloux has argued, the relationship between food and language changed in children's literature and conduct books from a figurative to a literal level by the late nineteenth century. In popular literary genres, food shifted from being a metaphor for words to an equation with language. Mailloux impressively demonstrates that by the 1890s it had become commonplace for authors to advise their readers, as Annie H. Ryder did in *Go Right on Girls!* (1891), "to digest your books, turn them into nourishment, make them a part of your life that lives always" (133–57).[5]

Crane was writing within an established tradition, then, when he used food to create an impression of depth—what he called a "braver inside"—contrasted with realism's surfaces and "outside look." When Maggie wonders how Pete dined, her imagination points upward, signalling transcendence of home, the slum, individual powerlessness, and a dog-eat-dog universe. *Maggie*, the novel itself, points downward, feeding readers' interests in how the poor literally starved and figuratively hungered for the refined and safer existence which Maggie envisions and the average reader already enjoys. Whether one adopts the vantage point of reformer or novelist, photographer or reader, the point of view is privileged; reality is observed from on high. How then does a reader avoid replicating the hypocrisy and self-deception which are blatantly attacked in the novel? As an example of 1890s social realism, Crane's challenge in *Maggie* was to make readers consume a text, not merely gaze at or patronize social issues raised by the text. The aesthetic challenge was to cause readers to make a text part of their selves as though they had eaten it, not to allow readers to dine elegantly on literary fare. However, the solution was not without problems, and Crane soon leapt from the frying pan into the fire. In breaking the planes of realism by imagining his words as food, Crane created new difficulties in the way his texts were consumed. As will be shown, problems with voyeurism yielded to problems about consumption.[6]

Chapter XV graphically demonstrates how the text *Maggie* might be read voyeuristically, that is, read much the way Mary in this chapter turns her daughter into spectacle. "Lookut her! Lookut her!" Mary shouts nine times in succession. Expounding "like a glib showman at a [sideshow] museum," she draws a "doorful of eyes" that gaze upon Maggie, their gaze objectifying her, proving her powerlessness. Even a "baby, overcome with curiosity concerning this object," crawls near to gaze (48), personifying Crane's fear that his novel may be read in an infantile way, or that the text might remain nothing but spectacle. Rather than empathizing with and absorbing the vision, a reader might remain mere spectator, mere voyeur, like Pete stuck merely on shapes, attracted only to form and surface. It is no surprise that the text avenges itself upon Pete by reversing the motif; surface yields to savagery as Pete's supposed friends pick him apart cannibalistically in a kind of devourment that is as far removed from voyeurism as can be (54).

The depth of the anxiety represented in these scenes could be missed by modern readers less steeped in humanistic background and reform impulse than were the realists. But the major source of the anxiety under study here is how realists, seeking a cure for realism's weaknesses, find that the cure is intricately connected with the problem; devourment is intimate with voyeurism. Dunbar certainly constructs that problem in *The Sport of the Gods* when Skaggsy and *The Universe* set Berry up, as Dunbar says, to "taste all the bitterness." As a realist, Dunbar replicates the crushing racist powers of life; it is no wonder that his preacherly voice so often intrudes to wish that life and the text could be other than realistic. When the choreographer, an arranger of music and dance if not words on a page, is shown to dislike the taste of his own words, one wonders how much Dunbar intends him self-reflexively to be an emblem of the realist author (547).

My contention is that, for Crane, the problem was more about ontology and aesthetics than humanism, closer to photography and the problem of the Other.

(...)

The two most obvious signals in *Maggie* are the stove and the saloon. The stove's first and literal function, of course, is for feeding the family as well as for warmth. Symbolically it functions as the urban surrogate for the domestic hearth, the psychological site where the family is supposed to center, as it does for the "hurrying men" in Chapter XV who do not notice the "forlorn woman" because they have "their thoughts fixed on distant dinners" (46). But for the Johnsons, that basic function fails; the stove is treated disgracefully, as when the supposed head of the family plops "his great muddled boots on the back part" (8). Although massive, or at least the heaviest object in the home, it takes a beating, sometimes bounced around as though it were made of cardboard instead of iron. It is also the site of the characters' only effort at art when Maggie, attempting to give her family class and to attract Pete's courtship (and thus start another family centered at its own stove), makes "with infinite care" (20) a lambrequin of alternate wheat and roses for the shelf above the stove. Her choice of pattern indicates her humble desire to combine simple food with plain beauty, and her future efforts to restore the lambrequin to its place create sympathy. Her longing for art is also lonely in this harsh environment. Pete does not notice the lambrequin, and the mother of the family destroys it in one of her drunken rampages.[11]

Most of all, the stove stands no more chance against the saloon than the past has against the future. As in George's Mother where the saloon's fraternity attempts to be a surrogate mother, the barroom offers a substitute family in the midst of an urban chaos that is as fragmented as the collars and cuffs in Maggie's workplace. As Riis wrote, "in many a tenement-house block the saloon is the one bright and cheery and humanly decent spot to be found" (79).[12] In Maggie's Chapter XI, alienation is commented on in a fittingly oblique way with a stranger whose presence seems as irrelevant to the text as it is in the tavern. The first time he is mentioned, Pete is "bending expectantly toward" him, but each of the next six times the stranger appears he is farther from the center of the bar. Finally, he is "sprawled very pyrotechnically out on the sidewalk" (37), and the usual crowd of spectators is there to gawk.

Notes

1. Unless otherwise noted, page numbers in parentheses in the text refer to Gullason's Norton Critical Edition (NCE), which is more readily available than Bowers's Virginia Edition.

4. A century later, the reality of starvation is so powerful that a popular writer depicting the depravity of slum life in 1992 also resorts to a mythic language of devourment. In his crime thriller *A Dance at the Slaughterhouse*, Lawrence Block compares the ghetto to the mythic Greek titan Cronus: "We are devouring our children, a whole generation of them. Wasting them, trashing them, throwing them away. Literally devouring them, in some cases" (139–40).

5. The most interesting modern theory that blends food and language is Louis Marin's *Food for Thought*, which depicts transubstantiation as a representation of the belief that words can transform reality just as they change bread into flesh in the Catholic ritual of communion, it is curious to see American Protestant reformers, many of them Protestant ministers, taking a view of food and language that Marin would consider Catholic. Scholarship that treats food primarily as a social phenomenon is voluminous, the most recent interesting treatment being Harvey A. Levenstein's *Paradox of Plenty*. See also Furst and Graham, eds., *Disorderly Eaters*.

6. In this sense, *Maggie*, as another of Crane's "Experiments in Misery," textually mirrors real-life pastimes. Americans like Walter Wyckoff would spend two years among the working class indulging in what looks to modern eyes like dilettantish curiosity. Some even labeled their adventures "an experiment in reality." See John Kasson, and Alexander Alland.

11. Ahnebrink reports Thomas Beer's claim that the lambrequin, along with the saloon fight, were the only two episodes taken directly from life (90); Joseph X. Brennan has an interesting discussion of the lambrequin.

12. The diseased, alcoholic world of *Maggie* has been much discussed. As a sampling, see Marston LaFrance, Alice Hall Petty, and Gerard Sweeney.

In Stephen Crane's *Maggie: A Girl of the Streets* (1893), it is possible to read the decline of the nineteenth-century mental philosophy of "character" and the rise of a modern psychology of "self-esteem." Crane's novel represents some of the first volleys fired in what Warren Susman calls "one of the fundamental conflicts of twentieth-century America": a "profound clash between different moral orders," "between two cultures—an older culture, often loosely labeled Puritan-republican, producer-capitalist culture, and a newly emerging culture of abundance" or consumption.[1] With Maggie, Crane sets out to reinvent the slum novel, and he proceeds in a programmatic fashion.[2] The novel is a *tour de force*, a kind of counter-demonstration. He takes a familiar tale, keeps the plot, but redoes the characterizations or the mental action as well as the moral judgment—to get the story right.[3] And it is significant that Crane chooses the representation of the lower classes for his battle ground; he could rewrite the motives of human behavior in any setting (and he would choose many), but the Bowery gave him something extra. Crane perceives in the turn-of-the-century slums, not vice, but an alternative morality—and moral inspiration. The slums had generally appeared to the middle class as a moral foil, an ethical morass short on character; Crane discovers there instead a more advanced culture of consumption and a heterodox hero of self-esteem, the swaggering Bowery tough.[4]

Crane chose for his plot an "old story" in the literature of the slums, as Frank Norris noted in review.[5] In fact, *Maggie* recounts the same basic tale as Edgar Fawcett's novel *The Evil That Men Do* (1889) and also shares compelling resemblances with Reverend Thomas de Witt Talmage's *Night Sides of City Life* (1878) and Charles Loring Brace's *The Dangerous Classes of New York* (1872)—depending on whether one reads Maggie's death scene as suicide or homicide.[6] Like Maggie, Fawcett's Cora is a slum girl subjected to the hardships of violent parents and menial labor; she is made love to and abandoned by a man, and she ends up a prostitute and then a corpse (Cora is murdered by a corrupt and unsavory brute).[7] According to Talmage, a fallen woman must choose between the cold garret of a sewing girl and the East River; Brace includes a drawing of a woman who is about to throw herself into the same river Maggie approaches in her last moments.[8]

It is as if Crane is saying to his pious colleagues, yes, you got the basic plot elements, the basic action correct, but you completely misunderstand how it comes about. Your mental philosophy is bunk; this is not a story about temptation, fall, and remorse, but rather intimidation, self-doubt, and self-loathing. Yes, says Crane in *Maggie*, the slum girl has premarital sex. Yes, she becomes a prostitute. Yes, she eventually kills herself or is murdered—Crane may be so deliberate in his attempt to set the record straight that he purposefully leaves Maggie's death ambiguous in order to cover both variants of this stereotypical story. In any case, for Crane, the rough outline of the action is correct, but everything else is mistaken. The details of the sexual behavior are wrong: Maggie is not tempted and seduced, and not by a playboy of an upper class; she falls for a Bowery tough. The sexual ethics of the slum are misunderstood: there is a portion of Crane's Bowery that has no prohibition against premarital sex. The girl's inner experience is misrepresented: because her values do not correspond to those of the middle class, Maggie experiences no temptation, no sense of sin, and no remorse for her sexual activity; rather, she is awed by a tough because he is, in her ethics, a moral exemplar. Finally, she becomes suicidal, not because of mounting guilt over her fall, but because of a progressive loss of self-esteem; she is not tough enough herself to make it in her slum world.

In the usual slum story of the late nineteenth century, the slum is a hothouse of vice, brimming with temptations, and the protagonist undergoes an internal moral transformation as she succumbs to her passions or transcends them with her will. Crane, then, rejects the standard characterization of the slum, the current mental philosophy of the middle class, and its concomitant model of the interaction between the individual and the environment. For him, the slum is not filled with temptations that seduce the passions, but insults that threaten pride. The slum is not an evil place but a separate moral universe, whose alternative ethics have developed in response to its inferior social status and physical misery. The people who populate the slums have not fallen into sin or risen above temptation; they have either hardened against the hardship and humiliation of their circumstances, or they have sunk into self-loathing. In fact, *Maggie*—once more programmatic—tells both of these new stories: Crane shows Maggie's brother Jimmie developing a healthy belligerence and Maggie falling into self-hatred. The central facts of human interiority are not character and the passions, but self-esteem and hostility. And the internal action of the slum story is therefore not alteration in character, but transformation in confidence.

The cornerstone of nineteenth-century mental philosophy was the supremacy of the moral sense over all other parts of the mind. As Thomas Upham put it in his popular textbook *Elements of Mental Philosophy* (1845),

> the moral sensibilities ... hold, in our estimation of them, a higher rank than the appetites, propensities, and passions....
> The moral sensibility appears to hold ... the position of a consultative and judicial power; it stands above ... and over ..., in the exercise of a higher authority; it keenly scrutinizes the motives of action; it compares emotion with emotion, desire with desire; it sits a sort of arbitress, holding the scales of justice, and dispensing such decisions as are requisite for the due regulation of the empire of the passions.[9]

Conscience, the moral sensibility, was supposed to act as a judicial power; its decisions were to be executed by the will. Moral character was practiced or habitual will; John Dewey explains in his *Psychology* (1886) that "character ... is will which ... has turned its force in one direction."[10] If good, character was then something like conscience automatized in will. The character—or the conscience with the aid of the will—was to control the passions and appetites; this was the ethical relationship one was to maintain with oneself.

(...)

Crane's genesis of the Bowery tough is not the stuff of Upham's mental philosophy. He does not portray the streets of lower New York as sites of moral infestation that his characters wisely avoid or resist or, conversely, that insidiously poison them or slowly wear down their spiritual immune systems. He does not adopt the metaphors of a moral epidemiology as do other novelists at the time. He does not, like Fawcett, claim that "human grossness ... spawned" in the tenement, or, like Sullivan, describe a boy "whose budding character had suffered from a poisonous moral atmosphere."[23] Rather, Crane portrays the tenement neighborhood as hostile and threatening and shows his character steeling himself against it.

Jimmie's inner experience in the slums is not one of temptation, sin, and guilt; it is one of insult, self-defense, and belligerence. He does not give in to surrounding temptation and then, like Fawcett's Cora, develop an "armor against remorse"; he is simply "hardened" against a hostile environment. His soul is "clad ... in armor" against the external world, "in defense." Jimmie struggles to preserve a sense of worth and superiority as he is subject to the abuse of drunken parents, the insults of religious missionaries, the spectacle of wealthier and better-dressed men, and the insurmountable powers of the police. He becomes a "man of leather"; he turns "his sneer ... upon all things"; he feels "obliged to quarrel"; he considers himself "above" Christians and aristocrats; he imagines that his "down-trodden position ... had [an] element of grandeur" (13–16).

The soul that Crane refers to here is not the ethical substance of mental philosophy.[24] To say that Jimmie "clad his soul in armor by means of happening hilariously in at a mission church where a man composed his sermon of 'yous'" is to imagine a different kind of soul. It is impossible for soul here to mean "character" or "conscience. First of all, Jimmie has walked into a church, a place where character or conscience thrives and therefore would have no reason to protect itself, Crane makes it absolutely clear that Jimmie's soul is not at home here. More fundamentally, it makes no sense to say that character is clad in armor, because character is itself armor— against temptation—that either holds or corrodes and gives. Character is that which withstands, fends off, or, through weakness, gives in to temptations and passions. And, as we saw with Fawcett's Cora, conscience is hardly in need of armor: it is pictured as an offensive weapon, against which one arms oneself, to protect oneself from the pain of remorse. What needs to be clad in armor is something soft, and here something vulnerable to a "sermon of 'yous'": the preacher is calling Jimmie and the other "sinners" and telling them, "you are damned" (13). Soul here refers to something like deep or intimate feelings about oneself. This is the sort of ethical substance that needs armor against the preacher's sermon. The armor, meanwhile, that protects self-esteem is belligerence: Jimmie happens in on the preacher "hilariously," which is to say, full of hostile mockery.

Notes

1. Warren Susman, *Culture as History* (New York: Pantheon, 1984), xx. As Susman puts it, "the older culture ... demanded something it called 'character,' which stressed moral qualities, whereas the newer culture insisted on 'personality,' which emphasized being liked and admired" (xxii). Where Susman talks of "a culture of personality" (271–85), I talk about an ethics of self-esteem. I might have used other words, such as self-respect, egotism, conceit (all words Crane also uses); I choose "self-esteem" because I want to indicate a link between Crane's ideas and our own contemporary moral-psychological perspective.

2. Crane's inability to find a publisher for *Maggie* is one indication of his success—especially when one considers that there was at the time a slum fiction fad, when certain books about the poor became veritable bestsellers (for example, Edgar Townsend's *Chimmie Fadden* [New York: Lovell, Coryell, 1895]).

3. As is well known, the novel's most obvious difference was that it lacked the preaching that was obligatory in slum literature. Though he describes sweatshop drudgery and tenement disorder, he does not sound the traditional charity themes of vice and crime, filth and disease, unhealthy and unsafe labor practices. There is Crane's well-known claim that "an artist has no business to preach"; we know, he boasts to his friends that "you can't find any preaching in *Maggie*." The novels of his contemporaries were for him "pink valentines." But the absence of preaching is only the beginning of what makes Crane's book unusual (R. W. Stallman, *Stephen Crane: A Biography* [New York: George Brazilier, 1968], 73, 79).

4. Crane's turn-of-the-century Bowery is a more advanced culture of consumption, obviously not because it is wealthier than middle class neighborhoods, but because it has far less interest in production—very little belief in hard work paying off—has fewer qualms about pleasure and indulgence, and, of critical importance, has access to a new world of mass-market goods.

5. Frank Norris, "Stephen Crane's Stories of Life in the Slums: *Maggie* and *George's Mother*," in *Maggie: A Girl of the Streets*, ed. Thomas Gullason (New York: W. W. Norton & Co., 1979), 151.

6. Maggie's death has been a source of contention in Crane criticism, and some critics have insisted on murder. Hershel Parker and Brian Higgins have maintained that the text to which most critics refer, the 1896 edition, a second published version of the book put out by a commercial company called Appleton, is unintelligible on the issue. In fact, they claim that it is only confusions in the somewhat expurgated 1896 version that have led readers to suspect that Maggie commits suicide, whereas she is actually murdered: by "a huge fat man in torn and greasy garments" who appears only in the 1893 edition (Hershel Parker and Brian Higgins, "Maggie's 'Last Night': Authorial Design and Editorial Patching," in Gullason, [note 5], 239). But homicide is merely implied in the 1893 version, and is no more definite than the suicide of the 1896 text: the reader sees no murder and is only told that "chuckling and leering, he [the fat man] followed the girl of crimson legions" (53). An argument could reasonably be made, from the 1893 edition, that Maggie is a suicide: she does, after all, walk into increasingly bad parts of town, while her garments suggest that she is not driven by urgent financial need. The text is simply not explicit about how she dies.

7. Edgar Fawcett, *The Evil That Men Do* (New York: Belford, 1889).

8. The reference to Talmage is in David Halliburton, *The Color of the Sky* (Cambridge: Cambridge Univ. Press, 1989), 68. Charles Loring Brace, *The Dangerous Classes of New York* (New York: Wynkoop & Hallenbeck, 1872).

9. Thomas Upham, *Elements of Mental Philosophy*, 2 vols. (New York: Harper, 1845), 2:23, 24–25.

10. Dewey goes on: "The man with character, whether good or bad, is not easily daunted. He does not recognize obstacles.... Weakness means instability, and instability is lack of character" (John Dewey, *Psychology* [New, York: Harper, 1898], 415).

23. Fawcett (note 7), 88; Sullivan (note 13), 17.

24. Ethical substance is Michel Foucault's term. Foucault calls the ethically relevant part of oneself "the ethical substance ... the individual has to constitute this or that part of himself as the prime material of moral conduct" (Michel Foucault, *The Use of Pleasure*, trans. Robert Hurley [New York: Pantheon Books, 1985], 26).

CHRISTOPHER BENFEY ON CRANE'S ARTISTIC DESCRIPTION OF THE MEAN STREETS

There is internal evidence as well for its early conception, for *Maggie* hardly reads like a researched and documented novel. What urban texture the novel manages to muster is borrowed from Riis and from Methodist tracts about the evils of the modern city. The rest of the novel, and the best of it, is all hypothesis, speculation, dream. *Maggie* apparently served as a preliminary sketch for what Crane expected to find in the city. His newspaper sketches—"The Men in the Storm," "Experiment in Misery," and the like—flesh out *Maggie*, rather than the reverse. The novel's influence on the course of Crane's life extended still further. For in his idealized portrait of a prostitute he was already imagining the kind of fallen women whom he later sought out, first in the streets of New York, and then in the aptly named Hotel de Dream.

Maggie is experimental in another sense as well. It takes risks with a familiar subject, boldly cutting new patterns out of old cloth. Crane chose a theme that invited sentimentality – the fall of an innocent slum girl into prostitution and suicide. The challenge was to play a new song on this battered instrument, handed from author to author in the nineteenth century, discarded by Zola, taken up by the English writer Arthur

Morrison in his book *Tales of Mean Streets,* and now making the rounds of American writers of reformist and sentimental fiction.

Crane probably thought his material would prove more innovative and shocking than it did. After all, he had spent far more time among the novel-burning Methodists of the Jersey shore than among world-weary New Yorkers. He may even have feared prosecution for writing pornography when he had the novel published in 1893, at his own expense, under the deliberately colorless and relative untraceable pseudonym "Johnston Smith." But reviewers were quick to point out that Crane's characters were already, as the novelist Frank Norris noted, "old acquaintances in the world of fiction." The hackneyed plot, to be sure, is simple enough. Maggie and Jimmie grow up in the slums. Their father dies and their mother drinks. Maggie is seduced by Jimmie's friend Pete. He ditches here and she becomes a prostitute. Jimmie and her mother kick her out of the house. She dies in the river.

Perhaps the very familiarity of the material appealed to Crane, though not from some modernist drive to "make it new." It would be more accurate to say that Crane made these materials *old.* Like a jazz musician toying with a "standard," he seems confident that we know the tune. He slows down some passages, takes others in cut time, and still others—like the exact circumstances of Maggie's death—he leaves out altogether. To contemporary reviewers the book seemed unfinished. But this sketchlike quality is ultimately part of Crane's argument. The lives he describes are fragmentary, built up of discordant parts, caught in a city that refuses to hold together.

Crane often seems to be building rather than simply observing his urban world; he makes it up as he goes, out of walls and stairs and fire escapes. It is fitting that his opening scene, when Maggie is a child, takes place on a heap of gravel—dumped there, presumably, to make or repair a street. And Maggie, we are told, "blossomed in a mud-puddle"—as much a product of the street as her brother, Jimmie. For these children, the streets are safer than the buildings that line them.

The tenements are not, like the uptown brownstones of Edit Wharton or Henry James, refuges of domestic privacy. They are dangerous "dark regions," sites of incessant violence and rampage.

The street is an appropriate stage for all Jimmie's roles. The king-of-the mountain game that opens the book has an almost comic energy. Jimmie is fighting for the "honor of Rum Alley" —his street identity. Crane describes this battle as a primitive rite, the children swearing "in barbaric trebles" and "fighting in the modes of four thousand years ago." It is as though the patrician wish for a "strenuous" life in the 1890s, which Teddy Roosevelt and his friend Frederic Remington imagined in the West, were available right here, a trolley-car ride away. The political anxiety among the uptown classes was that these urban warriors would rise up and take American society by force from the flabby aristocrats. It was in this context that Frederick Law Olmsted conceived of Central Park as a way to defuse urban hostilities.

Like the dangerous roughs that Olmsted and other reformers worried about, the teen-aged Jimmie begins hanging out on street corners.

He menaced mankind at the intersections of streets.

On the corners he was in life and of life. The world was going on and he was there to perceive it.

Not content to be a spectator, he soon takes a job as a truck driver, a lord of the streets who despises mere "foot passengers" and yields only to the sublime color and noise of fire trucks. And the women Jimmie favors are of course women of the street, whom he can treat with the same bullying disdain that he accords pedestrians.

A major theme in Maggie is the different status of "boys of the street," like Jimmie, and "girls of the street," like his sister. A young man hanging out on street corners is a spectator, a *flâneur*, taking in the passing scene, while a woman doing the same thing is something altogether different. As long as

Jimmie's friend Pete, the seductive bartender, accompanies Maggie through the streets, appearances are preserved. But once she wanders the streets alone she becomes fair game for any passing man. As Crane depicts him, Pete is nothing but appearance: he is the embodiment of the city-as-disguise. He's a slick talker and a slicker dresser, with "his blue double-breasted coat, edged with black braid, buttoned close to a red puff tie." The bar where he works is a little shrine to fakery and illusion.

The interior of the place was papered in olive and bronze tints of imitation leather. A shining bar of counterfeit massiveness extended down the side of the room. Behind it a great mahogany-appearing sideboard reached the ceiling. Upon its shelves rested pyramids of shimmering glasses that were never disturbed. Mirrors set in the face of the sideboard multiplied them.

Maggie, once she has emerged from her childhood "disguise of dirt," is of course taken in by all of Pete's fakery, and her destiny is to become herself a person of illusion and façade, "one of the painted cohorts of the city." When she turns to a minister for help, she finds that he too is concerned only with facades, with "saving his own respectability" instead of her soul.

DAVID HALLIBURTON ON THE SIGNIFICANCE OF THE COLOR YELLOW

Yellow led a lively life in the 1890s. This was the decade in which the telephone yellow pages and "yellow journalism" were launched. In 1895 Pulitzer's New York *World*, the paper that in the following year published Howells's review of *Maggie*, pictured a girl in a yellow dress, hoping that this experiment in color printing would attract more readers. To boost circulation for his own New York *Journal*, William Randolph Hearst hired R.F. Outcault away from Pulitzer, whereupon the graphic artist produced the Yellow Kid, the protagonist of the first sequential comic strip employing balloon dialogue. Meanwhile, in 1894, Aubrey Beardsley and Henry Harland, wanting to launch a trendy magazine, looked to the yellow covers in which French novels had long appeared, and transferred that hue to their own, producing *The Yellow Book*. A year earlier Crane published "Why Did the Young Clerk Swear?" the protagonist of which secretly reads a French novel; the drift of the action takes on a coyly erotic aspect as Crane transfers the traditional yellow, slightly altered, to his hero's moustache: "Soon it could have been noticed that his blond mustache [sic] took on a curl of enthusiasm ..." (VIII, 34).

In the same year, at his own expense, Crane published *Maggie*. Its covers were yellow.

It is one of the first colors to appear in the novel: "Over on the island a worm of yellow convicts came from the shadow of a grey ominous building and crawled slowly along the river's bank" (p. 5). Even as these people beyond the law foreshadow Maggie's illicit future, the juxtaposition of their yellow with the dark building foreshadows the crucial juxtaposition of yellow and black in Chapter 17, to be discussed below. Whatever yellow may look like when it occurs in Goethean purity, dust is one of those dull and coarse surfaces on which the color produces the kind of effect Goethe has mind: "A wind of early autumn raised yellow dust from cobbles and swirled it against an hundred windows" (p. 12). When a little later the "rough yellow" of the face and neck of Maggie's mother "flared suddenly crimson" (p. 17), and she swills "from a yellow-brown bottle" (p. 20), we see that she belongs to the same pattern.

For some time Maggie remains apart from the pattern of contamination and degeneration. For, though she "blossomed in a mud puddle" (p. 41), she avoids being muddied: "None of the dirt of Rum Alley seemed to be in her veins. The philosophers, upstairs, downstairs, and on the same floor, puzzled over it" (p. 41).

The color with the peculiar character is associated with the feelings of Maggie and the other employees, who are "of various shades of yellow discontent" (p. 42). In its next application the color adumbrates more: The "yellow silk women" (pp. 56, 59) are professional performers who, while they do not quite belong to the painted cohorts, are associated with drink and sex and hence contamination.

On two notable occasions Crane devotes attention to yellow glare. The same kind of excessive lighting, and especially glaring effects, had drawn the attention of Poe. In "The Philosophy of Furniture" Poe condemns glare as a leading error of decoration, and denounces the American infatuation with gas and glass and "the rage for glitter," suggesting that the mirror, "potent in producing a monstrous and odious uniformity," be banned altogether.[21] Crane for his part depicts the illumination in connection with illusion. To appreciate the effect it is necessary to quote at some length.

> On a corner a glass-fronted building shed a yellow glare upon the pavements. The open mouth of a saloon called seductively to passengers to enter and annihilate sorrow or create rage.
> The interior of the place was papered in olive and brown tints of imitation leather. A shining bar of counterfeit massiveness extended down the side of the room. Behind it a great mahogany-imitation sideboard reached the ceiling. Upon its shelves rested pyramids of shimmering glasses that were never disturbed. Mirrors set in the face of the sideboard multiplied them. Lemons, oranges, and paper napkins, arranged with mathematical precision, sat among the glasses. Many-hued decanters of liquor perched at regular intervals on the lower shelves. A nickelplated cash-register occupied a place in the exact centre of the general effect. The elementary sense of it all seemed to be opulence and geometrical accuracy. (pp. 91–2)

The description works on a variety of levels. Like the blue of "The Blue Hotel," the yellow glare publicizes the position of the saloon, assisting in the seduction of customers by attracting their attention. The glass front that makes this possible initiates a chain that includes the shimmering glasses inside, the nickel plate of the cash register, the shining bar, and everything that is also a mere front, such as the imitation leather, the counterfeit massiveness, and even the face of the sideboard with its imaging mirrors.

Since nearly everything in the description is manufactured, from the glass to the cash register, it is tempting to attribute the illusionary effects to artifice. But the natural and the artificial, interwoven in the same color spectrum, are not easily distinguished. In the present case there are the lemons and oranges, which are cousins of the yellow in the opening paragraph. Earlier, on the lambrequin in the Johnson flat may be seen "immense sheaves of yellow wheat and red roses of equal size" (p. 85), and then there is Pete's glitter and glory at the far, "transcendental" end of the spectrum, where the artifices of his manner inspire Maggie to see in him the ultimate natural object of the world: "Swaggering Pete loomed like a golden sun" (p. 68).

The second and last yellow glare occurs at the end of Chapter 17 as Maggie finds herself beside the horrible red fat man:

> At their feet the river appeared a deathly black hue. Some hidden factory sent up a yellow glare, that lit for a moment the waters lapping oilily against the timbers. The varied sounds of life, made joyous by distance and seeming unapproachableness, came faintly and died away to a silence. (p. 149)

After the deathly black hue of the river brings attention down, up goes the yellow glare, whereupon attention comes back down once more to the waters. The concluding sentence, by contrast, works on a horizontal plane as sounds come from distant venues. Here the visual and the aural are interwoven: The black is visual; the yellow, though visual in itself, illuminates the sight and sound of lapping; while the aural dominates in the sounds that die away to silence. The significance of all this for the protagonist is not far to seek.

After Maggie arrives at the final block, in the preceding paragraph, the tall buildings first appear, their eyes looking over her into the distance. Then, in the paragraph quoted above, there is a rising movement that falls in the end, followed by another rising movement that also falls in the end, followed by a sense of distance and the ultimate diminution—where sound is concerned—of silence. Here, in essence, is the structure of a dying fall.

Note

21. *The Complete Works of Edgar Allen Poe*, the "Virginia Edition," ed. James A. Harrison (New York: University Society, 1902), XIV, 128.

ALICE HALL PETRY ON WILLIAM HOGARTH'S INFLUENCE ON CRANE

Maggie is a tease. For decades now, literary historians and Crane scholars have attempted to ascertain the sources of this painful rendering of late nineteenth-century Bowery slum life, but the results have been far from conclusive. One school of *Maggie* source-hunters has assumed the literary approach, arguing that Crane drew his inspiration from Flaubert's *Madame Bovary*, from Zola's *L'Assommoir*, from such contemporary works as the Rev. Thomas DeWitt Talmage's *The Night Sides of City Life*, or even from Kipling's *The Light That Failed*.[1] There is some basis for all of these suggestions; but the fact remains that Crane was "unusually ill-read,"[2] and any attempt to proffer a specific literary text as the source of the content or technique of any Crane work must take this into account.

This caveat is especially prominent in the commentaries of the other school of Maggie source-hunters, those who assume the painterly approach. Drawing upon the incontrovertible facts that Crane's sister Mary Helen was a practicing artist and art instructor; that one of Crane's early loves (approximately 1888 to 1892) was Phebe English, a professional painter; that

Crane lived in the studios of several New York illustrators in the 1890s; and that several of his writings—including *The Third Violet*, "The Silver Pageant," and "Stories Told by an Artist"—focus specifically on artists, these commentators argue persuasively that "Crane's involvement with painting ... seems circumambient in his life."[3] The simple fact that Crane was personally quite familiar with the art world has generated several theories dealing with the ways in which various painterly techniques and movements might have affected the content or style of his fiction or, more broadly, his personal aesthetic. Some of these theories, such as R.W. Stallman's notion of "prose pointillism," are interesting but ultimately too subjective to be convincing. More substantial is the related, long-lived belief that Crane is best perceived as an "Impressionist." First suggested by such contemporary commentators as Joseph Conrad and Edward Garnett, the Crane-as-Impressionist theory argues that he was directly inspired by the French Impressionist painters of the nineteenth century. One hundred years later, critics such as James Nagel and Sergio Perosa continue, with provocative results, to explore Crane's fiction from the standpoint of Impressionist painting.[4] *Maggie* has had its share of Impressionistic readings; but I think it would be more fruitful to approach that grim tale not from the standpoint of the nineteenth-century French Impressionists but rather from that of the eighteenth-century English Realists. Specifically, I believe that an important pictorial source for *Maggie* was the famous 1751 engraving *Gin Lane*, by painter/illustrator William Hogarth (1697–1764).

Consider the opening of Crane's story: "A very little boy stood upon a heap of gravel for the honor of Rum Alley" (p. 7).[5] Joseph Katz notes that Rum Alley (and Devil's Row) "do not appear on official maps; they apparently bear constructed names which function symbolically in the novel." This sentiment is echoed by Thomas Gullason, who theorizes that "Rum Alley may have been suggested to Crane by the chapter, 'The Reign of Rum,' in Jacob Riis's *How the Other Half Lives*."[6] It seems far more likely that the name "Rum Alley" was directly inspired by the name "Gin Lane" and/or by the name of the

companion-piece of this engraving, "Beer Street" (1751)—
Hogarth's paean to the virtues of mild English ale. Even
Gullason's reference to Riis points ultimately to Hogarth, for
the English engraver's work had inspired a popular volume
entitled *Low-Life: or, One Half of the World, knows not how the
Other Half lives,* privately printed some time in the 1750s.[7]
Crane himself denied to Arthur Bartlett Maurice that he knew
the precise location of Rum Alley, but avowed that he "had
seen" it and that it "had haunted him and still haunted him."
Might he not have been "haunted" (consciously or otherwise)
by the memory of Hogarth's nightmare vision of Augustan
London[8]—a vision which bore startling resemblance to the
Bowery of the 1890s?

Both visions, after all, focus on two issues which touched
Crane deeply: slum life and intemperance. *Maggie* is now
regarded as the first American novel to depict urban slum life
artistically, and Hogarth's engravings performed a comparable
service for eighteenth-century London—so much so that a
controversy arose as to whether unpalatable engravings such as
Gin Lane even qualified as art. Charles Dickens himself was
struck by the degree to which *Gin Lane* "forces on four]
attention a most neglected[,] wretched neighbourhood, and an
unwholesome, indecent[,] abject condition of life"[9]—words
which could just as readily be applied to *Maggie*. More to the
point, much of the misery depicted in both Crane's and
Hogarth's works is directly attributable to the vicious cycle of
poverty and readily-available cheap liquor. *Gin Lane* was
Hogarth's personal contribution to the prohibition movement
in eighteenth-century England, and in fact *Gin Lane* was
credited with bringing about the so-called Tippling Act,
designed to curtail the sale of liquor in the British Isles. Not
surprisingly, *Gin Lane* for more than a century served as a sort
of pictorial temperance tract,[10] and it is plausible that Crane
first became familiar with Hogarth not through his
involvement with artists, but through his mother's work in the
Women's Christian Temperance Union.

One element of slum life and intemperance which
particularly appalled both Hogarth and Crane was the

breakdown of the family unit. The first half of *Maggie* reads like a social worker's case study: all three children—Maggie, Jimmie, baby Tommie—are either neglected or abused. Tommie in particular is a cipher. In the first family scene in the story, he is injured in a scuffle between Jimmie and his mother, but no one notices or cares. Tommie's death is particularly chilling in its brevity and abruptness: "The babe, Tommie, died. He went away in an insignificant coffin ..." (p. 20). The other Johnson children fare no better. Jimmie's father steals and drinks the liquor which the boy has purchased for a neighbor and then, laughing, hits his son on the head with the empty pail. Both Jimmie and Maggie—"Her features ... haggard from weeping, and her eyes gleam[ing] with fear" (p. 19)—must hide lest they awaken their drunken parents, exhausted from their latest violent quarrel. And of course it is her rejection by her family, as much as by Pete, which drives Maggie to prostitution: "'Go t' hell an' good riddance.' Maggie went" (p. 41). The world of Hogarth is as cruel to innocent children as is Crane's: at the center of *Gin Lane*, a half-naked infant boy helplessly falls head-first out of his drunken mother's arms, and is about to die on the pavement in front of a saloon; in the distance, immediately above the mother's load, a drunken man holding a bellows has inadvertently impaled a baby, whose posture is identical to that of the falling boy; immediately to the left of the man with the bellows, an orphaned baby cries as his mother is lifted into her coffin; at the far right of the picture, a woman pours gin into the mouth of her infant; and immediately behind her, two little charity girls toast one another with gin.

Notes

1. R.W. Stallman discusses *Maggie* and *Madame Bovary* in his *Stephen Crane: A Biography* (New York: George Braziller, 1968), pp, 77–78. For Zola's influence, see James B. Colvert's "Introduction" to the University of Virginia Edition of *The Works of Stephen Crane*, Vol. I: *Bowery Tales*, ed. Fredson Bowers (Charlottesville: Univ. Press of Virginia, 1969), pp. xliii–xlvi. The possible influence of Talmage and his contemporaries is discussed by Marcus Cunliffe in "Stephen Crane and the American Background of *Maggie*," *American Quarterly*, 7 (1955), 31–44. For a consideration of *The Light That Failed*, see Colvert, pp. xlvii ff.

2. James B. Colvert, "The Origins of Stephen Crane's Literary Creed," *University of Texas Studies in English*, 34 (1955), 181.

3. James Nagel, *Stephen Crane and Literary Impressionism* (University Park: Pennsylvania State Univ. Press, 1980), p. 17. For Crane and Phebe English, see Joseph J. Kwiat, "Stephen Crane and Painting," *American Quarterly*, 4 (1952), 332. For Crane and the New York art scene, see Eric Solomon, *Stephen Crane: From Parody to Realism* (Cambridge: Harvard Univ. Press, 1966) and Corwin K. Linson's *My Stephen Crane*, ed. Edwin H. Cady (Syracuse: Syracuse Univ. Press, 1958).

4. See R.W. Stallman, *Stephen Crane: An Omnibus* (New York: Knopf, 1961); Joseph Conrad's remarks in *Stephen Crane: Letters*, ed. R.W. Stallman and Lillian Gilkes (New York: New York Univ. Press, 1960), pp. 154–56; Edward Garnett, "Mr. Stephen Crane: An Appreciation," *Academy*, 55 (1898), 483–84; Nagel, *Stephen Crane and Literary Impressionism*; and Sergio Perosa, "Naturalism and Impressionism in Stephen Crane's Fiction" in *Stephen Crane: A Collection of Critical Essays*, ed. Maurice Bassan (Englewood Cliffs, N.J.: Prentice-Hall, 1967), pp. 80–94.

5. I follow the text of *Maggie* in the University of Virginia Edition. Page references are indicated parenthetically in the body of the paper.

6. Katz, ed., *The Portable Stephen Crane* (New York: Penguin, 1969), p. 4, n. 2; Gullason, ed., *Maggie: A Girl of the Streets* (New York: Norton, 1979), p. 3, n. 1.

7. See Austin Dobson, *William Hogarth* (New York: Dodd, Mead, 1891), pp. 204–05.

8. Maurice, *The New York of the Novelists* (New York: Dodd, Mead, 1916), p. 107. Writes art critic Derek Jarrett, "few people who saw Hogarth's image of the gin-sodden mother with her baby falling from her arms ever forgot it. To this day it remains one of the most enduring and familiar of all our glimpses of eighteenth-century life" (*The Ingenious Mr. Hogarth* [London: Michael Joseph, 1976], p. 146).

9. John Forster, *The Life of Charles Dickens* (London: J.M. Dent, 1927), II, 42.

10. For a melodramatic nineteenth-century interpretation of *Gin Lane* as a pictorial temperance tract, see *The Works of William Hogarth* (London: J. Dicks [1874]), pp. 121–22. The details in the engraving are explained in *The Works of William Hogarth with Descriptions and Explanations* by John Trusler, John Nichols, and John Ireland (London: Simpkin, Marshall, Hamilton, Kent, n.d.).

James B. Colvert on *Maggie* as a Radically New Form of Conventional Writing

That stormy winter, as blizzard followed blizzard and the city lay smothered in thick snow, Crane was often at Linson's gloomy studio, lounging on a ragged couch covered with a rumpled blanket and surrounded by piles of old magazines and papers and dirty canvases. He was tinkering with *Maggie*, revising it in light of advice from Will and some of his friends. Will had complained that the absence of names for the characters—they were simply epithets like "the girl," "the mere boy," "the woman of brilliance and audacity"—was confusing. He suggested the change in the title and, incidentally, advised Crane to get it copyrighted. Wallis McHarg, a friend from boyhood days in Asbury Park, visiting on his way to Germany to study medicine, had read it with grave misgivings. It was a doubtful subject for literature, he had thought, and like Will he had objected to the anonymity of the characters.

By late February or early March the novel was ready, and he began showing it to editors. Willis Johnson of the *Tribune* was impressed by "the throbbing vitality and dynamics of the story" but warned him that it would be hard to find a reputable publisher since it would obviously "shock the Podsnaps and Mrs. Grundys" and "bring on him a storm of condemnation."[12] What other editors said is not known, but Johnson's view was undoubtedly typical, and Crane wasted little time trying to find a publisher after these first efforts. Impatient to see it in print, he sold stock in a Pennsylvania coal mine he had inherited from his mother, borrowed money from William, and ordered 1,100 copies of the book from a lower Sixth Avenue print shop. Johnson's warning had convinced Crane, as he wrote later, that it would be better to publish under a pseudonym, and he asked a friend, "what he thought was the stupidest name in the world." The friend suggested "Johnson or Smith and 'Johnston Smith' went on the ugly yellow cover of the book by mistake. You see, I was going to wait until all the world was pyrotechnic about Johnston Smith's 'Maggie' and then I was going to flop down like a trapeze performer from the wire and, coming forward with all the modest grace of a consumptive nun, say, I am he, friends! ..." The printing bill was $869, and he learned later that the print shop, which specialized in religious and medical books, overcharged him by about $700. "You may take this," he wrote someone, "as proffered evidence of my imbecility."[13]

The banal plot of the novel he was so eager to get before the public made *Maggie* more suitable, as it seems in broad outline, to sentimental melodrama than to literary art. It tells the story of Maggie Johnson, a young girl victimized by poverty and the viciousness of slum life. Her mother is the Amazonian Mary Johnson, well known in police courts for her frequent drunken rampages. She alternately beats her children and smothers them with maudlin demonstrations of affection. The brooding, indifferent father protests the beatings because they disturb his peace. The sickly baby, Tommie, dies of abuse and neglect. Jimmie, Maggie's younger brother, grows up to become a truck driver who bullies the world from the high seat of his van, bawling curses and threats at pedestrians and other drivers. He lounges on street corners with Pete, a swaggering bartender who at sixteen wears the "chronic sneer of an ideal manhood." Jimmie introduces Pete to the blossoming Maggie, who sees in the bartender a fascinating man of the world, admirable for the awesome power of his fists and his masterful knowledge of the ways of the streets. The mother accuses Maggie of yielding to Pete's sexual advances and drives her out of the tenement, outraged, as is Jimmie, by her affront to their respectability. Maggie accepts Pete's protection, but he quickly tires of her, and when he turns her out, she drifts into prostitution. One evening, in a mood of despair, she turns away from the bright avenue where she plies her trade, makes her way through dark streets to the river, and drowns herself. When Jimmie brings the news to their mother, she bawls tearfully to the assembled women of the tenement, "Oh yes, I'll fergive her! I'll fergive her!"

(...)

The plot of *Maggie* is a fabrication of elements drawn from this familiar pattern of themes, ideas, and attitudes. The characters (the pure, betrayed Maggie who "blossomed in a mud puddle" only to fall victim to her heartless seducer, drunken parents, and vicious brother), the attitudes (the author's scorn of "respectable" people, his assumption of Maggie's essential innocence), the action (the fights, the suicide), and the attribution of causes (alcohol, social determinism, the hypocrisy of the respectable world) are the basic elements of the stereotypical plot. Edgar Fawcett had used the plot in his 1889 novel of the slums, *The Evil That Men Do*, more than two years before Crane began *Maggie*. Cora Stang, the heroine in Fawcett's novel, is "a delicate blushing-rose in the midst of ... smirk and soilure," and though she aspires to be "a flower of sinless and beautiful love," she is seduced and abandoned, victimized by "the savage forces of birth, heredity, and poverty." She is scorned by respectable people of "egoistic indifference" who "murder philanthropy," and her brief career as a prostitute ends tragically in her murder.

What saves *Maggie* from the inherent banality of the well-known story is Crane's treatment. The "phrase-by-phrase concentration, the steady brilliance, and the large design," as John Berryman says, reflect the conception of art that "initiated modern American writing."[18] In method, he is radically new. He casts aside the familiar devices and conventions of fiction; he abandons customary narrative order and tells the story in a series of loosely related episodes. He makes few concessions to literal realism, presenting the tenement world in a constant flurry of images that seem to refer less to its objective reality than to its effect on the feelings and ideas of the characters. A looming tenement house is displaced in time and space, seen dreamlike with its "hundred windows" and "dozen gruesome doorways" that give up "loads of babies to the street and gutter" while "withered persons ... sat smoking pipes in obscure corners."[19] The short, simple sentences abound in odd turns of phrases, unexpected metaphors, revelations of strange perspectives. A saloon squats on a corner, its open mouth calling seductively. All things seem to be projections of someone's hopes, desires, and fears. Walking the avenue, Maggie the prostitute encounters "a stout gentleman, with pompous and philanthropic whiskers, who went stolidly by, the broad of his back sneering at the girl." "The picture he makes," Norris wrote perceptively, "is not a single carefully composed painting, serious, finished, scrupulously studied, but rather scores and scores of tiny flashlight photographs, instantaneous, caught, as it were, on the run."[20] *Maggie* is hardly an example of social realism, despite Crane's declared allegiance to the doctrines of Howells and Garland. Deeply indebted as it was to commonplace social myths, it seemed altogether innovative, as Garland acknowledged when he wrote later that Crane "had the genius which makes an old world new."[21]

Notes

12. Willis Fletcher Johnson, "The Launching of Stephen Crane," *Literary Digest International Book Review* 4 (April 1926): 289.

13. Beer, 90–91.

18. John Berryman, *Stephen Crane* (New York: William Sloane, 1950), 52.

19. *Works*, vol. 1, 11.

20. Norris, 13.

21. Hamlin Garland, "Stephen Crane: A Soldier of Fortune," *Saturday Evening Post*, 28 July 1900, 16.

CHESTER L. WOLFORD
ON THE MYTH OF PERSEPHONE

Whatever else it may be, *Maggie* is Crane's first sustained attempt at putting together classical materials in a modern form. The novel is more than a paradigm of naturalism and more than the parody of the sentimental slum novel Eric Solomon suggests;[4] part of the naturalism of *Maggie* is the determinism of tragedy, and the significant parody focuses upon a displacement of classical myth—an inversion of the Persephone/Proserpina myth driven with such a nihilistic force that the normal conservative limits of parodic intention are set aside.

A "voracious reader" of the classics, Crane could have encountered the Persephone myth in many places, but most likely in Ovid. Ovid's account describes Proserpina, the virgin daughter of the harvest deity Ceres, as picking flowers in a woodland meadow-garden that surrounds a pool with eternal spring and sunshine. Suddenly, Dis, dread god of the underworld, comes through the pool driving a chariot. In a flash he sees, loves, rapes, and carries the hapless ex-virgin back through the pool to Hades. Missing her daughter, Ceres lays waste the land in a frenzy of fear and lamentation until informed of Proserpina's whereabouts. Ceres then races to Jove for arbitration. He finally decrees, according to one account, that Proserpina must henceforth divide her time between earth and hell.[5] In short, it is a season myth, a Greek and Roman pagan Genesis of death and rebirth.

Crane inverts this myth. Instead of Proserpina's hopeful, fecund, rural spring, Maggie's season is a despairing, sterile, urban "autumn [which] raise[s] yellow dust from cobbles and swirl[s] it against an hundred windows" (1:11). Maggie spends her childhood peering from comers into a "dark region" of "frantic quarrels" where cooking odors fill the "darkening chaos of backyards" with "smoke" and "steam" and the "hiss" of boiling potatoes (1:11–14). Full darkness ironically illuminates an even greater horror; for then, should the demon called "mother" awaken, "all the fiends would come from below" (1:19). Maggie's father says it outright: "Home reg'lar hell" (1:17).

Such as they were, childhood and adolescence end early. By the fifth chapter, the father and the "babe," Tommie, have died; brother Jimmie has grown up "hardened," and "the girl, Maggie, [has] blossomed in a mud puddle." Beauty, however, provides no way out, only the choice between the hells of the sweatshop and the street.

The possibility that Proserpina's pool is here turned into Maggie's mud puddle is less important to the myth's displacement than the fact that like Proserpina, Maggie is identified with flowers. Unlike Proserpina, Maggie spends all of her life in a sort of hell, and she is therefore associated with flowers in a way that inverts the original myth's intention. Instead of symbolizing the fecundity of life, flowers are associated with death.[6] Maggie's method and purpose in picking flowers, for example, contrast markedly with Proserpina's: Tommie "went away in an insignificant coffin, his small waxen hand clutching a flower that the girl, Maggie, had stolen from an Italian" (1:20).

When she first sees Pete, her eventual lover, Maggie looks at him as a flower might first view the sun. She initially becomes aware of his presence through "half-closed eyes" (1:25) which open like blooming flowers ultimately to behold a "golden sun" (1:35), a Sol, who departs from their first meeting in "a sort of blaze of glory" (1:27–28). Her natural feelings of inferiority before this sky-god are similarly conveyed through flower imagery. Before their first date, she finds "the almost faded flowers in the carpet-pattern" to be "newly hideous" (1:28). In an effort to make her home more presentable for him, she buys "flowered cretonne for a lambrequin" (1:28). Her mother gets drunk and tears the lambrequin, so that Pete arrives to find its "knot of blue ribbons" looking like "violated flowers" (1:29). Emotionally and physically violated at home and in the factory, where she feels herself "shrivelling" (1:35) in the heat, Maggie increasingly looks towards Pete as a more natural source of warmth and as a way out of the burning hells of home and work. Knowing that "the bloom upon her cheeks" (1:35) will fade some day, she yearns to bask in the warmth of the sun.

Pete is opposite from what Maggie thinks he is. He is not Sol, but rather the Bowery equivalent of Dis. Part of Pete's "courtship" of Maggie, for example, the trip to the Museum of Arts, may be taken for a guided tour through Hades. Here Maggie wanders through "vaulted rooms" guarded by "watch dogs," while Pete describes a display of mummified remains: "Look at all dese little jugs! Hundred jugs in a row! Ten rows in a case an' 'bout a t'ousand cases!" (1:36). Even Dis is amazed that death has undone so many. Maggie's mother, Mary Johnson, identifies Pete in Christian terms when she throws

Maggie out of the house: "Yeh've gone t' d' devil, Mag Johnson.... Go t' hell wid him, damn yeh, an' good riddance. Go t' hell an' see how yeh likes it" (1:41).

Maggie goes, and for a time she likes it. Pete is a bartender and a sort of Bowery king, for it is he who receives alms and dispenses oblivion. The palace of his kingdom is the bar, and here all his subjects, including Maggie, are treated to fine Saturday nights. The saloon is a liquid Circe's isle, a place, too, where sirens sing "seductively to passengers to enter and annihilate sorrow or create rage" (1:45). Those places Pete takes Maggie have a liquid, misty underwater effect, creating a near parody of classical hells. The bar is filled with jars of pickles "swimming in vinegar" and "many-hued decanters of liquor" (1:45). In another beer hall there is a moist "smoke cloud" that "eddie[s] and swirl[s] like a shadowy river" (1:57).

Outside the barrooms, Pete is still associated with Hades, particularly at crucial moments in his relationship with Maggie. After Mary packs them off "t' hell," Maggie asks Pete if he loves her. His reply: "O, hell, yes" (1:42). When he abandons her, he says, "Go to' hell" (1:67). Yet when he reflected upon this act, "he did not consider that he had ruined Maggie," or that "her soul would never smile again," just as Dis failed to dwell on whether Proserpina would be happy in Hades. In hell, "souls did not insist upon being happy."

Notes

4. Eric Solomon, *Crane: From Parody to Realism*, p. 23.

5. Ovid, *Metamorphoses*, bk. 5, lines 341–570. Since Ovid's account is used here, I use the Roman names for the gods in discussing *Maggie*.

6. A remarkable parallel to *Maggie* occurs in Puccini's *La Bohème*, the libretto for which was written in 1896. The heroine, Mimi, is similarly poor, forced to prostitute herself, and associated with flowers in the midst of the urban squalor of Paris. Further, both *La Bohème* and *Maggie* are naturalistic works which work hard at exposing the pathos of unrealistic perceptions of life. Unlike *Maggie*, however, *La Bohème* is apparently based on a minor French novel written in 1844.

JOSEPH X. BRENNAN
ON CRANE'S USE OF IRONY

Perhaps the most remarkable single characteristic of *Maggie* is its insistent, and at times even oppressive, ironic tone. In its sustained and almost vehement irony *Maggie* was as much without precedent in American fiction as in its daring subject matter, and even today, in spite of all that the school of naturalism has produced in this manner, Crane's short narrative still marks something of the limits to which the method can go. In *Maggie*, indeed, the irony is so all-pervasive, ranging from the inversion of a single word or phrase to the thematic idea itself, that it is at once the most striking and yet most elusive aspect of the novel. In order to illustrate better how far-reaching this irony is, I shall proceed generally from its more overt and localized to its more complex manifestations, from the ironic cast of the single word or phrase to the ironic manipulation of theme and character.

Of the ironic inversion of the single term one might cite numerous instances; chapter iv, however, provides several of the more interesting examples. In the second paragraph of this chapter we read that Jimmie "studied human nature in the gutter, and found it no worse than he thought he had reason to believe it." Where we would ordinarily expect "no better" Crane overreaches our expectations to emphasize not only Jimmie's cynicism but the inversion of his scale of values as well: in his world there is no concept of good and bad; there is only bad or worse. This ironic twist is reinforced in the next sentence as well: "He never conceived a respect for the world, because he had begun with no idols that it had smashed." And later in this chapter, when Jimmie, by his premeditated indifference, had successfully snarled traffic, we read that "some blue policeman turned red and began ... to ... beat the soft noses of the responsible horses." Quite clearly the responsibility was not the horses'; Crane achieves an ironic effect here, however, not by a mere arbitrary inversion of the expected but by momentarily abandoning his usual objectivity and letting, as it were, the policeman's red point of view prevail.

The same might be said for Crane's ironic use of the term "reverently" in the last sentence of this chapter: "Nevertheless, he had, on a certain starlit evening, said wonderingly and quite reverently, 'Deh moon looks like hell, don't it?'" This entire passage, indeed, following immediately upon a terse review of Jimmie's brawlings and seductions, is itself a trenchant ironic commentary upon his soulfulness and sensitivity.

More interesting yet, in chapter xvi, is Crane's use of the word "respectability" as a kind of ironic motif; the term is repeated six times, each time with broadening implications and heightened ironic effect. There is a very deliberate progression here—from Pete's apprehension lest Maggie should compromise the "atmosphere of respectability upon which the proprietor insisted"—the term being used three times in this association—to his confused impression that the respectability of the barroom now, being threatened is really his own respectability. Having driven Maggie away at last, Pete then returns "with an air of relief, to his respectability," so that the psychological transference from the barroom to himself is now complete. In the last paragraph this motif reappears when a picture of benevolence and kind-heartedness to whom Maggie makes a gesture of appeal for help draws back from her convulsively to save his respectability. Thus in the brief course of this scene, by means of an ironic manipulation of the term, Crane reduces respectability to a hypocritical sham, a convenient justification for cruelty, irresponsibility, and indifference.

In the delineation of the main characters, moreover, Crane employs with telling effect a technique of ironically leveling the reader's normal assumptions and expectations. When we first encounter Jimmie in chapter i, for example, he is the "little champion," fighting against overwhelming odds for the honor of Rum Alley. But lest by his initial display of courage he should too seriously engage our sympathies, a short while thereafter he turns his fists with unabated fury upon his defenseless sister. In chapter iii, when the father snatches the can of beer which Jimmie had just bought for the leathery old woman downstairs, he protests as though from a certain sense of justice, "Ah, come off! I got dis can fer dat ol' woman, an' it 'ud be dirt teh swipe it. See?" But a moment thereafter we perceive that he is really more concerned with the difficulties this creates for himself: "Look at deh dirt what yeh done me.... Deh ol' woman'll be t'rowin' fits." Similarly one might be led to expect that the mother's objection to Jimmie's fighting springs from some dim instinct of solicitude for his physical well-being, yet, as it turns out, the real reason for her objection is that he tears his clothes. One wonders, too, when the father shouts at Jimmie, "Leave yer sister alone on the street," whether it is to Jimmie's pounding of Maggie or to the publicity of it that he is really objecting. In short, Crane has a real flair for this sort of ironic qualification of proper appearances with improper and unexpected motives; by means of this device he can deeply compromise his characters with one deft economical stroke.

Works by Stephen Crane

Maggie, A Girl of the Streets, 1893.

The Red Badge of Courage, 1895.

George's Mother, 1896.

The Third Violet, 1897.

Active Service, 1899.

The O'Ruddy (with Robert Barr), 1903.

The Works of Stephen Crane 12 vols. (Wilson Follett, ed.), 1925–1927.

The Works of Stephen Crane 10 vols. (Fredson Bowers, ed.), 1969–1976.

The Complete Short Stores and Sketches of Stephen Crane (Thomas A. Gullason, ed.), 1967.

The Complete Novels of Stephen Crane (Thomas A. Gullason, ed.), 1967.

Stephen Crane: Prose and Poetry (J.C. Levenson, ed.), 1984.

The Correspondence of Stephen Crane (Wertheim and Sorrentino, eds.), 1988.

Annotated Bibliography

Ahnebrink, Lars. *The Beginnings of Naturalism in American Fiction: A Study of the Works of* Hamlin Garland, Stephen Crane and Frank Norris, *With Special Reference to Some European Influences, 1891–1903.* New York: Russell & Russell, 1961.

A classic work on the emerging American literary naturalism of the 1890s, Ahnebrink discusses Crane's pessimistic view of man, with special emphasis on Zola's determinism. Maggie and Jimmie are prototypically weak and uncomplicated characters who are meant to illustrate the doctrine of the affliction brought about by evil heredity and a impoverished, urban environment.

Benfey, Christopher. "Mean Streets" from *The Double Life of Stephen Crane.* New York: Alfred A. Knopf (1992): 55–79.

Benfrey discusses *Maggie* in the context of certain crucial biographical facts—the death of his mother in 1891 and the "intensive spurt" during which Crane claimed to have written *Maggie*, the challenge of writing about slum life in New York *before* he had any direct experience of the city, and his characterization of Maggie as a dreamer like himself.

Bergon, Frank. "Crane's Sense of Story" from *Stephen Crane's Artistry.* New York and London: Columbia University Press (1975): 63–100.

Bergon focuses on *Maggie* as a novel distinct from Crane's earlier stories, which provided Crane with the opportunity to create an artistic rendition of a realistic and socially important subject. Bergon maintains that Crane's prose is designed to "arouse and excite sensations," a style which will lead the way to a real understanding of slum life in New York City.

Berryman, John. "New York." From *Stephen Crane.* New York: William Sloane Associates, Inc., (1950): 51–96.

Citing Crane's remarks to a friend in 1893, Berryman suggests that Crane's particular notion of realism is actually impressionism, a means of getting at the truth. Berryman lauds Crane's literary contribution in *Maggie* as an endeavor both daring and ambitious, a work "of intense pressure and nearly perfect detachment."

Brennan, Joseph X. "Ironic and Symbolic Structure in *Maggie*." From *Nineteenth-Century Fiction* 16, no. 4 (March 1962): 303–15.

Brennan focuses on the subtlety and calculated artistry in *Maggie* in which the central irony dramatizes the condemnation of a woman by the same society that produced her downfall. Brennan maintains that Crane's use of irony is unprecedented in American fiction in its consistency and pervasiveness, and demonstrates numerous instances of ironic inversion on both the level of individual words and phrases and the interlinking of chapters.

Cady, Edwin H. "Crane's Art before *The Red Badge of Courage*." From *Stephen Crane*. New York: Twayne Publishers (1962): 96–114.

Cady discusses *Maggie* as a work of realism, a doctrine which Crane derived from Howells and Garland. Cady states that *Maggie* demonstrates Crane's early achievement of style with its pictorial power, accuracy of speech, setting and type, as well as Crane's defiance of his contemporary, genteel censors.

Colvert, James B. "New York." From *Stephen Crane*. San Diego: Harcourt Brace Jovanovich (1984): 39–78.

Colvert discusses *Maggie* within in the context of important biographical facts concerning Crane's life and journalistic career in New York. He focuses on the ways in which *Maggie* is radically new from conventional writing on the evils of slum life, among them Crane's use of episodic storytelling rather than customary narrative order, and the transformation of literal realism into an impressionist flurry of images which emphasize emotional effects rather than what is literally seen.

Gandal, Keith. "Stephen Crane's "Maggie" and the Modern Soul." From *ELH* 60, no. 3 (Fall 1993): 759–85.

Gandal reads *Maggie: A Girl of the Streets* as a departure from the late nineteenth-century slum novel in which "character" is guided by conscience and transformed by means of a moral struggle. Gandal identifies two opposing psychological types that represent the moral soul: Jimmie's defensive and belligerent posture against slum life and Maggie's progressive weakening into self-doubt.

Gibson, Donald B. "Crane Among the Darwinians." From *The Fiction of Stephen Crane*. Carbondale and Edwardsville: Southern Illinois University Press (1968): 25–39.

Gibson maintains that Crane's purpose is to protest the Darwinian universe, rather than either supporting or rejecting his theories. Gibson sees Crane's nonjudgmental, yet extreme, application of Darwin as leading to inconsistencies and contradictions in *Maggie*, whereby he is not justified in assigning culpability to any of his characters as they are all unwitting victims of their environment.

Golemba, Henry. "'Distant Dinners' in Stephen Crane's Maggie: Representing "The Other Half." From *Essays in Literature*, vol. XXI, no. 2 (Fall 1994): 235–50.

Golemba discusses the language of food as an expression of the reality of starvation in 1890's slum life. Golemba maintains that Crane's challenge was to get his readers to experience both literal and figurative hunger by causing them to "consume the text," rather than observing Maggie from a privileged vantage point.

Gullason, Thomas A. "The Prophetic City in Stephen Crane's 1893 *Maggie*." From *Modern Fiction Studies* vol. 24, no. 1 (Spring 1978): 129–37.

Gullason discusses *Maggie* as a pivotal work in the history of both the city novel and the American novel by treating slum life and social problems as worthy of serious attention in a work of fiction. Gullason reads *Maggie* as a material-spiritual tragedy which "weighs the terrible and tragic price of city life."

Gullason, Thomas A. "Tragedy and Melodrama in Stephen Crane's *Maggie*." From the Norton Critical Edition of *Maggie: A Girl of the Streets*." New York and London: W.W. Norton & Company (1979): 245–53.

Gullason identifies two competing "genres" in *Maggie*, tragedy versus melodrama. He grants a limited Aristotelian sense of tragedy in the representation of fear and pity, absent any truly heroic and noble characters, and the melodramatic mode of *Maggie* in which sensation, violence, mawkish sentiment and vulgar rhetoric predominate.

Halliburton, David. "Conflict as Condition: *Maggie: A Girl of the Streets*." From *The Color of the Sky: A Study of Stephen Crane*. Cambridge and New York: Cambridge University Press (1989): 38–70.

Halliburton discusses *Maggie* in the context of conflict as the irremedial condition of existence in the slums where characters live in a state of wonder closely akin to shock. Halliburton does a very close reading of the novel in terms of characterization and cultural details, discussing a broad range of perspectives. Using a variety of comparative and interdisciplinary methods, he gives a detailed discussion of such themes as the function of the grotesque, the Johnson family in contrast to other inhabitants of the Bowery, the lack of compassion and the significance of color imagery.

Hakutani, Yoshinobu. "Jennie, Maggie, and the City." From *Dreiser's Jennie Gerhardt: New Essays on the Restored Text*. Edited by James L.W. West III (1995): 147–56

Hakutani contrasts the unabating victimization of Maggie Johnson and family with Dresier's portrayal of family life in *Jennie Gerhardt*. Hakutani sees Crane's depiction of Bowery life as extremely confining, imposing a paralysis from which its residents cannot break free, whereas Dreiser's portrayal of urban life is one in which the characters are able to transcend the destructive reality of the urban slum.

Krause, Stanley. "The Surrealism of Crane's Naturalism in *Maggie.*" From *American Literary Realism* 16, no. 2 (1983): 253–61.

Defining the supernatural as a "situation in which life begins to parody itself," Krause locates the supernatural in the ambiguity of Crane's naturalism. He maintains that Crane's naturalism is so severe, that the real becomes subsumed by the "blackness of its unreality," rendering the wish for transcendence an impossibility.

Petry, Alice Hall. "Gin Lane *in the Bowery: Crane's* Maggie *and William Hogarth.*" From *American Literature* 56, no. 3 (October 1984): 417–26.

Emphasizing various artistic and social influences in Crane's biography, Petry identifies Hogarth, an eighteenth-century English Realist and satirical artist, as an important source for *Maggie.* Citing many compelling facts, Petry maintains that Hogarth's "Gin Alley" provided a vision of the mental and physical degeneration the family unit as well as the irresponsibility of the Church which became the foundation of Crane's novel.

Pizer, Donald. ""*Maggie* and the Naturalistic Aesthetic of Length." From *American Literary Realism 1870–1910*, vol. 28, no. 1 (Fall 1995): 58–65.

Pizer identifies three basic aspects of naturalistic fiction: the naturalistic writers association of length as a means to accepting the environment as destiny; the assumption the mass is of greater than the individual; and the importance of social detail. Pizer finds that the issue of brevity is a distinctive and idiosyncratic form of naturalism in *Maggie* whereby Crane is able to encapsulate the notion of social causality..

Pizer, Donald. "Stephen Crane's 'Maggie' and American Naturalism." *Criticism* 7 (1965): 168–75.

Pizer discusses the ways in which *Maggie: A Girl of the Streets* clashes with conventional expectations of naturalistic fiction. Among the many characteristics which make Crane's novel unique are his use of irony and Maggie's function "as an almost expressionistic symbol of inner purity" that remains unsullied despite her ugliness of slum life.

Robertson, Michael. "*Reporting the City*: New York Journalism." From *Stephen Crane, Journalism, and the Making of Modern American Literature*. New York: Columbia University Press (1997): 75–113.

Robertson identifies Crane's dual career as journalist-novelist as part of an emerging central myth in modern American literature of the 1890s where young reporters on assignment in city streets observed the grim reality of urban slum life. Nevertheless, Robertson maintains that Crane's achievement in *Maggie* is far more complex than a simple progression from journalistic observation to fiction.

Wolford, Chester L. *The Anger of Stephen Crane: Fiction and the Epic Tradition*. Lincoln and London: University of Nebraska Press, 1983.

Wolford discusses Crane's early attempt to blend myth and tragedy with naturalism in *Maggie* without incorporating the classical elements of epic of the hero, both more than human and all too human, must take decisive action for a mistake he has made. Wolford maintains that Maggie Johnson's biggest mistake is that of being born, and the novel itself reverses tragedy in that offers no final optimism.

 Contributors

Harold Bloom is Sterling Professor of the Humanities at Yale University. He is the author of over 20 books, including *Shelley's Mythmaking* (1959), *The Visionary Company* (1961), *Blake's Apocalypse* (1963), *Yeats* (1970), *A Map of Misreading* (1975), *Kabbalah and Criticism* (1975), *Agon: Toward a Theory of Revisionism* (1982), *The American Religion* (1992), *The Western Canon* (1994), and *Omens of Millennium: The Gnosis of Angels, Dreams, and Resurrection* (1996). *The Anxiety of Influence* (1973) sets forth Professor Bloom's provocative theory of the literary relationships between the great writers and their predecessors. His most recent books include *Shakespeare: The Invention of the Human* (1998), a 1998 National Book Award finalist, *How to Read and Why* (2000), *Genius: A Mosaic of One Hundred Exemplary Creative Minds* (2002), and *Hamlet: Poem Unlimited* (2003). In 1999, Professor Bloom received the prestigious American Academy of Arts and Letters Gold Medal for Criticism, and in 2002 he received the Catalonia International Prize.

Janyce Marson is a doctoral student at New York University. She is writing a dissertation on the rhetoric of the mechanical in Wordsworth, Coleridge, and Mary Shelley.

Michael Robertson is the author of "Stephen Crane's Other War Masterpiece" and "An Ironist at the Seashore: Possible Additions to the Crane Canon" with David Holmes and Roxanna Paez.

Donald Pizer has been a professor of English and American Literature at Tulane University. He is the editor of *The Cambridge Companion to American Realism and Naturalism: Howells to London, Critical Essays on Stephen Crane's The Red Badge of Courage* and the author of *American Expatriate Writing and the Paris Moment: Modernism and Place* and *Twentieth-Century American Literary Naturalism: An Interpretation.*

Henry Golemba has been a professor of American Literature at Wayne State University. He is the author of *Thoreau's Wild Rhetoric*, *George Ripley*, and *Frank R. Stockton*.

Keith Gandal has been an associate professor of English at Northern Illinois University. He is the author of *The Virtues of the Vicious: Jacob Riis, Stephen Crane and the Spectacle of the Slum* and "Stephen Crane's 'Mystic Places.'"

Christopher Benfey has been a professor of English at Mount Holyoke College. He is the author of *The Great Wave: Gilded Age Misfits, Japanese Eccentrics, and the Opening of Old Japan*, *Emily Dickinson: The Lives of a Poet* and *Degas in New Orleans: Encounters in the Creole World of Kate Chopin and George Washington Cable*.

David Halliburton is Professor Emeritus of Comparative Literature at Stanford University. He is the author of *The Fateful Discourse of Worldly Things*, *Poetic Thinking: An Approach to Heidegger* and *Edgar Allan Poe: A Phenomenological View*.

Alice Hall Petry has been an associate professor of English at the Rhode Island School of Design, a visiting professor at the University of Colorado, Boulder, a Fulbright Scholar at the Federal University of Paraná in Brazil, and a Senior Postdoctoral Fellow of the American Council of Learned Societies. She is the author of *Understanding Anne Tyler* and *A Genius in His Way: The Art of Cable's Old Creole Days*.

James B. Colvert is Professor Emeritus of English at the University of Georgia. He is the author of "Stephen Crane and Postmodern Theory," "Stephen Crane: Style as Invention," "Stephen Crane's Magic Mountain," and "Ernest Hemingway's Morality in Action."

Chester L. Wolford has been a professor of English at Pennsylvania State University. He is the author of *Stephen Crane: A Study of the Short Fiction*, *"The Red Badge of Courage*

Mocks the Greek Epic," and "The Eagle and the Crow: High Tragedy and Epic in 'The Blue Hotel.'"

Joseph X. Brennan has contributed his essay on ironic and symbolic structure to the Norton Critical Edition of *Maggie: A Girl of the Streets*. He has also published other essays on Crane.

Acknowledgments

"*Reporting the City*: New York Journalism" by Michael Robertson. From *Stephen Crane, Journalism, and the Making of Modern American Literature*. New York: Columbia University Press (1997): 75–76. © 1997 by Michael Robertson. Reprinted by permission.

"*Maggie* and the Naturalistic Aesthetic of Length" by Donald Pizer. From *American Literary Realism 1870–1910*, vol. 28, no. 1 (Fall 1995): 58–9 and 61–3. © 1995 by McFarland & Company, Inc. Reprinted by permission.

"'Distant Dinners' in Stephen Crane's *Maggie*: Representing 'The Other Half'" by Henry Golemba. From *Essays in Literature*, vol. XXI, no. 2 (Fall 1994): 235; 237–9 and 242–3.) © 1994 by Western Illinois University. Reprinted by permission.

"Stephen Crane's 'Maggie' and the Modern Soul" by Keith Gandal. From *ELH* 60, no. 3 Fall 1993): 759–61 and 765–6. © 1993 by The Johns Hopkins University Press. Reprinted by permission.

"Mean Streets" by Christopher Benfey. From *The Double Life of Stephen Crane*. New York: Alfred A. Knopf (1992): 63–66. © 1992 by Christopher Benfey. Reprinted by permission.

"Conflict as Condition: *Maggie: A Girl of the Streets*" by David Halliburton. From *The Color of the Sky: A Study of Stephen Crane*. Cambridge and New York: Cambridge University Press (1989): 63–5. © 1989 by Cambridge University Press. Reprinted by permission.

"Gin Lane *in the Bowery*: Crane's *Maggie and William Hogarth*" by Alice Hall Petry. From *American Literature* 56, no. 3 (1984 Oct.): 417–421. © 1984 by the Duke University Press. Reprinted by permission.

"New York" by James B. Colvert. From *Stephen Crane*. San Diego: Harcourt Brace Jovanovich (1984): 46–53. © 1984 by James B. Colvert. Reprinted by permission.

Index

M

Madame Bovary, (Flaubert), 67
Madison Square Garden, 9
Maggie, Johnson, (main character in *Maggie*), 39, 44, 73, 76–77, 81
  abandoned by Pete, 35
  her death, 37–38
  her downfall, 24
  on escaping her poverty, 21, 24, 29, 32
  her first date with Pete, 30–31
  and homeless, 36
  her infatuation with Pete, 29, 63
  and life of prostitution, 37
  her sad life, 7
  her trust in Pete, 33–34
  on trying to improve her world, 29–30
Maggie: A Girl of the Streets
  the color yellow, 64–66
  as experimental novel, 60–61
  the fight, 26, 46–47
  irony in, 41, 44, 79–81
  naturalism in, 43, 75
  and nighttime at the Bowery, 33
  the plot, 15, 73–74
  prose of, 41
  and published anonymously, 16, 61, 72
  related to Crane's journalism, 40–42
  the saloon, 52–53
  slum life in, 26–27
  the symbol of the stove, 52
  on urban slum, 69
  voyeurism in, 50–51
  vulgarity in, 15–16
  words as food, 50
Mailloux, Steven
  on food and language, 50
Mary, (character in *Maggie*), 73, 77–78
  her alcoholism, 26, 30
  her failure as a parent, 32–33
  on Maggie's death, 38

and mother of Maggie and Jimmie, 24–25
Maurice, Arthur Bartlett, 69
May, Phil, 16
McCabe, James D. Jr., 17
McHarg, Wallis, 72
McNamara, Brooks
  on the Atlantic Garden, 17–18
Melodrama, 21–22
Melville, Herman, 14
Men in the Storm, The, (story), 60
Metropolitan Museum of Art, 19, 23
Miss Smith, (character in *Maggie*), 25
Monroe, Hersey, 15
Monroe, Lily Brandon
  her affair with Crane, 15
Morrison, Arthur, 60–61
Mould, Jacob Wrey, 22

N

Nagel, James, 68
  on naturalism and impressionism, 45
Nell, (character in *Maggie*)
  her relationship with Pete, 35–37
New Jersey Coast News Bureau, 41
New Testament, 49–50
New York City Police Department, 8
New York Journal, 8, 10, 63–64
New York Tribune, 40–41
New York World, 10
  the color yellow, 63
Night Sides of City Life, (Talmage), 54, 67
Norris, Frank, 54, 61, 75
  on slum literature, 39–40
Nut-Brown Maiden, 12

O

Old Testament, 49–50
Olmstead, Frederick Law, 22, 62
O'Ruddy, The, 14
Outcault, R.F., 63–64